KU-207-279

WINNING TALES FROM SCOTTISH HOUSES

WINNING TALES FROM SCOTTISH HOUSES

CANONGATE

First published in 1986
by Canongate Publishing Limited
17 Jeffrey Street,
Edinburgh, Scotland.

British Library Cataloguing in Publication Data

Winning Tales from Scottish Houses told
by their families: the best entries in
the Canongate Historic Houses competition.
1. Short Stories, English — Scottish authors
2. English fiction — 20th century
823 '.01' 089411 (FS) PR 8675

Cased ISBN 0 86241 133 5
Paperback ISBN 0 86241 117 3

Typeset by EUSPB, 48 Pleasance, Edinburgh.

Printed in Great Britain by
Biddles Limited, Guildford.

Contents

The Winner

The Macphersons of Ralia and Glentruim are directly descended from the younger son of the ancient house of Cluny Macpherson. The family has lived in the historic clan lands of Badenoch — between Loch Laggan and Aviemore, for almost a thousand years; Glentruim lies in the heart of this wild and rugged country.

In the early part of the century Euan Macpherson of Ralia went to live in Glentruim, three miles from his previous home. The building was a ruin and was rebuilt in 1826 in its present form, retaining some walls of the old house, once the home of the Duke of Gordon.

It was Lord Cockburn who remarked that Euan Macpherson had embarked on "a bold attempt to make a habitable residence in the most savage position of the whole Strath . . . but since he has the courage to begin and to live there I predict it being one day a fine and not uncomfortable Highland place".

Four Sons

Euan Macpherson

GLENTRUIM

The web of our life is of mingled yarn
good and ill together.
All's Well That Ends Well — W. Shakespeare

Angus Macdonald paused and then stopped. His thumb slid beneath the strap of the rifle on his shoulder and thrust it back into the position where it had lain before that last hard struggle through the deep snow. Being a gamekeeper at Glentruim like his father before him, he would usually never pause or stop to rest, but today was different. Today, between the ridges of heather burnt black by winter's frost, lay deep runnels of snow, remainders of the wild storms of winter so recently past. It was possible to walk across these wide drifts in the corries, since the surface generally was covered with wind-crust and stepping lightly and delicately the surface crust held. But then on the next step the surface broke and Angus, up to his thighs in the deep snow, struggled endlessly before he could gain the next foothold. The last drift had been particularly deep and treacherous and so it was that having won through to the first rocky ground of the ridge, he stopped to regain his breath.

The valley of the Upper Spey lay below him, the river winding tortuously along the floor of the valley bordered on each side by the arable fields which at last were showing the first faint hue of green. Across the valley the high hills of Glenshiro still held their mantle of snow sharply etched against the brilliant blue sky of that early day in spring. In the valley below him, the ewe flock was gathered in-bye in readiness for lambing — tiny dots of white in the pasture-land by the Spey.

Seeing them there reminded Angus of his purpose that day. Yesterday he had found fresh prints of foxes out on the hill, foxes which would come down from the hills at the start of lambing and play havoc amongst the flock. Hunting foxes in order to save the young lambs was a familiar task which he had performed each year for so many years that his skill as hunter had been sharpened by experience; he could smell a fox on the wind at half a mile and his sight rivalled that of the eagle flying high above.

He was just about to start again up the steep ridge below Eagle Rock when he heard the bell ringing below. It sounded shrill and clear in the frosty, sun-drenched landscape. It rang and stopped, rang again and so three times the bell sounded across the valley, then silence. He smiled quietly to himself and turned to look far below at the Woods of Glentruim which hid the castle, his own house and all the other cottages making up the tiny community of the families working on the estate. In his mind's eye he could picture the scene down there. Three rings of the bell above the coach house were calling Donald, the coachman, to stop his other work on the estate and run home to the coach house. Donald would be changing from his working clothes into black boots, white breeches, black jacket, white gloves, cravat and top hat. It was the time that Donald most enjoyed — other duties on the estate were only to be endured. Whilst Donald changed, the groom and stableboy would be harnessing up the coach and in the courtyard beneath Donald's bedroom window there would be the sound of horses' hooves and the grating noise of the coach wheels on the cobblestones below. It was a scene remembered from childhood when, if he was not out on the hill with his father, he would help young Donald, in those days the stablelad, but now the coachman, to harness the horses. That was in the old days when Evan was Laird. His son Lachlan, the present Laird, was a sterner man. He was fair and just but not as well loved as the old Laird. And so Angus stood as a statue on the mountain below Eagle Rock, his thoughts a kaleidoscope of memories of the past and joy in the present loveliness of that brilliant cold morning in spring.

When Angus at last moved again the fox did also. It had been lying in a hollow on the ridge in front of him and sprang up. For one brief moment they stood facing each other in silence. But in that moment Angus slipped the rifle from his shoulder, levelled and fired. The fox, poised with muscles taut in readiness to escape, leaped high in the air and fell. In the very place where moments before it had been basking in April sunshine the fox lay, the sun darkening in its eyes as death came.

In the valley hidden amongst the Woods of Glentruim the coach had started its journey to Balaville for the Lunch Party. Lachlan, the Laird, in Highland dress with bonnet crowned with the eagle feathers of Chieftain, sat silently beside his wife. Lady Glentruim sat warmly covered with fur rugs. The trees lining the avenue were already beginning to bud, but in the hollows untouched by the sun the rhododendron bushes lay in shadow still whitened by the frost of the night before.

At the South Lodge the coach stopped whilst the iron gates were opened. The horses stood still, their warm breath steaming from their nostrils with only an occasional impatient stamp of a hoof to break the silence. In that silence they heard the shot. It sounded across from Glentruim to the cliffs of Creag Dubh and echoed to and fro across the valley again and again.

Lachlan immediately thought of Angus. He could imagine in all its detail what at that moment was happening out on the hill. Angus would be quickly reloading and waiting with bated breath to see if the quarry rose again. And when no movement was seen Angus would go slowly forward, rifle at the ready, in case a second shot were needed. It rarely was. Of all the many times over so many years that he had been out on the hill with his gamekeeper he had never known Angus to miss a shot. Lachlan was inwardly a shy man who accepted the social chatter of a lunch party as a necessary part of his life, but would have preferred to be out in the high places of rock and peat bog, and the smell of heather. The appointment for lunch at Balaville had been made many weeks before, but if only today he could have dressed in old tweeds and been out with his stalking telescope on the hill with Angus.

It was late in the afternoon when the coach returned home on its five-mile journey from Balaville. Lady Glentruim went straight upstairs to rest and change before dinner. Lachlan went into the library and sat before the log fire burning in the huge hearth. His thoughts went back over the events of the day. In early morning he had sat here at his desk and one by one the estate workers had come in to discuss the work to be done that day. On the farm, since lambing was near, care and feeding of the ewe flock had first priority.

In the sheltered and walled garden preparation could now begin for planting spring vegetables. In the woods there were trees blown by winter storms to be cleared and cut in readiness for next winter's fuel and on the hill there were foxes, the predators of this year's lambs. He remembered the shot he had heard while waiting at the gates at the South Lodge. Tomorrow morning Angus would come in and tell of his day on the hill.

It was the governess who knocked quietly and came in to interrupt his reverie of the day's events. The boys were not to be found. They should have been home at four o'clock to spend two hours in the schoolroom but although she had looked everywhere for them they were not to be seen. She left with strict instructions that as soon as the boys returned they were to be sent straight to him.

He felt a sense of irritation that his well-ordered life should be disturbed by any unforeseen event. Such things should not happen and his sons must obey him at all times. Once or twice recently he had observed a certain rebelliousness which was altogether unhealthy and unnatural. It was undoubtedly the work of Evan, his oldest son, who since reaching his teens had somehow become quietly defiant towards him, his father. As minutes ticked by he felt anger welling up inside him and when, after half an hour his sons had still not reported to him, his slow anger burned more strongly. In a cupboard there was a tawse, a heavy leather belt, and quietly and very deliberately he took it from the cupboard and laid it on the green leather-topped desk in a far corner of the library.

Across the Spey Valley the sun had begun to set in fierce splendour. The oil lamps were lit and preparations for dinner were taking place with the dining room table set for Lachlan, Lady Glentruim and their six children. But still the four boys were nowhere to be found. Even as time passed Lachlan felt his anger turning to unease. Lady Glentruim went quickly from one to the other questioning, pleading. Yes, the boys had been there at lunch-time, had eaten well and were in good spirits, but had not been seen since. No, they had said nothing of their plans for the afternoon, after lunch they had gone out and had simply not been seen again. Each witness questioned, each answered in the same manner.

But now the minutes had fled into hours and darkness lay over the valley with the first stars beginning to appear and after the day of clear sky frost began to settle on the ground like iron. Lady

Glentruim with her daughters, Maria and Eva, went into the dining room but ate little. Lachlan stayed in the library, for once in his life hesitant and indecisive. Fear and anger still struggled within him. Fear finally prevailed and with it came decision. All the men from the cottages, the coachman Donald, Angus, the gardeners, farm workers from the Home Farm and the tenanted farms came quickly once the word was spread and stood silently outside the front door of Glentruim. Each man was issued with a torch and each received his instructions, where to search and how to search.

Lachlan Macpherson, father of the boys

As Angus Macdonald stepped forward to receive his flaming torch he felt a heaviness in his limbs after his long day in the hills and as great a heaviness within. He was filled with foreboding for the task ahead which he felt was doomed to failure. He thought of the dense tangle of the young pine woods which hid the wildcats whose presence he had so often sensed. Above the pines was the emptiness of the hills where even in daylight stags could be found only after a hard search through his stalking telescope. It was so difficult to find wildcat, fox, deer or any other living thing in these woods and mountains — what possible chance could there be, on this bitter night, of finding the four missing sons of the Laird?

Setting forth, he weaved his way backward and forward across the rough ground, stopping from time to time to shout the names of the boys, sometimes one name sometimes another, then stood, his ears straining to catch a distant answering cry. All he heard were the familiar sounds, the hollow murmur of a far-off mountain stream, the bark of a roe deer close by startled by his torch and his movement, and the eternal sound of wind across the heather. Eventually his torch spluttered and died. For long moments he stood utterly still. Throwing back his head he called once more each of the boys' names in turn. His voice sounded tiny and lost in the hidden corries of the mountains and starlit heavens above. Then, just before turning to retrace his steps, he whispered very low in his native tongue, "Cun cumadh Dia Fabhailte thu" — "May God keep you safe".

Lachlan began to ponder a succession of awful possibilities. The boys would often go out on the hill together to stalk deer. Not to stalk and kill, but simply to go quietly through the heather, crawling silently to see how close to the deer they could get before they were seen. Had they strayed too far across the moors and become exhausted and unable to make their way home? At this time of year the rivers had their first run of salmon — had they gone to the river? Perhaps one of them falling in the deep pools of the Truim had needed help from the others and they in turn had fallen and drowned. On the steep cliff face of the Tor he had been building steps up the rock face. They were forbidden to go there before the work was finished, but perhaps Evan had taken them there and, climbing the unfinished steps, they had fallen a hundred feet to the rocks below. Each vision more vivid and more frightful followed in succession. His wife, weeping, had retired, as had his daughters.

The doctor who came some time ago to assist had given them each a small dose of laudanam and sent them to bed.

Lachlan stood outside lighting his own torch and as he did his hand trembled with the chill of darkness. He walked in the starlit night through the dark pinewoods of Nessan Tulloch and came to the Falls of Truim. The river was swollen by the melting snows of Drumochter and his shouts were drowned by the torrents of water. In the deep pools below each of the falls, the light of his torch reflected across the surface of the water flashing back messages of light, but no message of hope. The pools were more than twelve feet deep and beneath the surface his sons could be lying undisturbed by the turbulent current across the surface. With a feeling of utter helplessness he retraced his footsteps home.

On the other side of the mountains in the valley of the Spey the other searchers calling out the names of the boys continued their quest. The torches darted back and forth along the banks of the river like fireflies. But finally the torches were gutted and died and one by one the men returned to report having found no trace. And as they did the weather started to change quite suddenly as it so often does in the Highlands. The sky clouded over and the wind turned to the north bringing with it quick, sharp flurries of snow. The men walked back shivering to their cottages, lamps were turned off and soon the only sound in the valley was of the bitter north wind stirring in Glentruim Woods.

Back in the library, Lachlan thought of the past hours since he had been there in the afternoon waiting for the governurse to send his sons to him. It seemed more than a lifetime ago. Then he was content, secure and happy. Now his whole life lay in ruins about him. His sons, for whom he had such high hopes and dreams, were gone. Tomorrow there would be the task of dragging the pools of the River Truim and the deep dark waters of the Spey. There was nothing that could be done now. He knew that he should go to comfort his wife but going to their bedroom door he heard no sound so he tiptoed downstairs again. This night he would not sleep. Even if the doctor had left laudanam for him he doubted if he could sleep then or, for many months to come, ever sleep again in peace.

The fresh log sparked and flamed in the dying embers of the fire. On the oval table in the centre of the room stood decanters and glasses and he filled a glass with whisky and sat again before the fire. He thought of his sons each in turn. Evan, strong-willed and rebellious, growing quickly and soon to be a man. Duncan, a year younger, quiet, at times too quiet, but always obedient. Norman, cheerful and full of mischief, amusement at almost everything in life lurking in his dark brown eyes. And Iain, so much younger than the others. He found it hard to talk to Iain as he did to the others. Iain was so close to his mother he felt out of reach to him. He thought of each and of all the many things they had done together. He was very proud of them. Although perhaps he was strict and could rarely demonstrate affection towards them he loved them as only a father can his sons.

The hours of night passed slowly, endlessly. Each time he threw a fresh log on the fire the flames leaped in the hearth and cast dancing shadows across the pannelled walls and bookshelves as he walked to the oval table to recharge his glass. It was the silence that finally broke into his thoughts. The wind with its low moan blowing round the Tower had quieted and in its place there was a stillness as if the whole world had suddenly held its breath. Lachlan went to the lighted windows peering out into the darkness. Now that the wind had dropped the snow was falling in thick, slow, heavy flakes blanketing the lawns below Glentruim. He shuddered with the

The desk at which Lachlan sat with his tawse and percussion revolver

certain realisation that no human being could ever survive such a night as this in the open.

And then he caught sight of the leather belt which he had placed carefully on his desk in readiness so long ago when his sons were still alive. The tears came, a bursting pressure in his chest and as again the embers in the hearth flickered and dimmed, grief overwhelmed him.

It was much later that with tear-stained face he saw the first grey streaks of dawn across the sky. The whisky decanter was empty and, carrying it in one hand, a candle in the other, he crossed the hall and his footsteps echoed in the silent house as he went down the stone stairway to the cellar. The cellars at Glentruim are below ground where the temperature never changes more than two degrees in winter or summer. He pressed the latch and in the dim candlelight passed the rows of dusty bottles lying sleeping in their racks. And then another door into the inner cellar. There were more rows of faintly shining bottles as he walked to where, directly in the centre of the room on its wooden trestle, stood the forty-five gallon cask of whisky which, by tradition, always stood in that place.

The floor was made of cobblestones, uneven beneath his feet. He took one step forward, stumbled, gasped, and in sudden fright lifted the candle high above his head to look down. Beneath the cask of whisky and lying at his feet in drunken stupor, were four bodies — his four sons. Evan, even in sleep, arrogant with arm flung carelessly above his head and resting against the wooden trestle. Duncan, deeply asleep, quietly composed. Norman, still with a mischievous smile tracing the corners of his lips. Iain, curled up with knees close to his chin. The hand holding the candle shook uncontrollably, he felt his heart pounding. He could only think, "My sons, my sons, my beloved sons."

Whether it was his footsteps as he ran back up the stone steps from the cellar ,or his shouts, or both, which woke the household, the whole house was soon awake. He did not know or think or care what he was saying: "I've found them — I've found them — my sons — the cellar, they're alive — I've found them."

All was bustle and haste. Hot water bottles were filled and the boys one by one carried gently up to their beds. Lady Glentruim, her eyes heavy with tears and drugged sleep, went from one to the other, to the other and the other and back to the first. The reality was so hard to grasp. She felt terror that she might wake and that what now had happened might on wakening turn out to be no more than a dream.

When all was done, in night robe she joined her husband in the library. They stood together at the window as dawn came with dark clouds still burdened with snow and whiteness carpeting the ground. Over to the east, above the Grampian mountains, there was a sudden break in the cloud and shafts of morning sunlight kindled the warmth of another day on the snow-covered branches of the pine trees below.

This is a true tale as it was told to me, but what happened the following day was never told and so I can only guess.

I like to think that the four sons slept late next day. Lachlan didn't go to bed and after his wife had left his side he sat on in the library with the fire of the night before still burning in the hearth. He felt a huge thankfulness and peace within him. At last he stood up and went to the leather-topped desk where the tawse still lay in readiness. He took it and once again went down the cellar stairs and hung it on a hook in the furthest corner of the inner room of the wine cellar.

This may be purely surmise — but how else can one explain the fact that to this very day, more than a hundred years later, in a corner of the wine cellar there hangs a tawse held still in the cobweb of time where it has been from that day to this?

Some Exploits of William Craik

Beauchamp Blackett

ARBIGLAND

The family of Craik lived on the Barony of Arbigland in Dumfries-shire from 1679 until 1852 when they sold the property to my forebears. Most of them left little mark on history or the district and unfortunately must have held a bonfire of family papers before moving out.

One, however, left an indelible mark locally, having built the present mansion, laid out the entire property and built Kirkbean Church during his ninety-five-year span. William Craik must have had a robust constitution since it was said of him that "he was never abed if there was light in the sky and considered it a scandal for any man to go to bed sober". He was one of the greatest of early agricultural improvers, and a pioneer of land drainage and husbandry.

It has always been a mystery how he managed to achieve all this whilst pouring money into the estate for very small returns.

Some years ago my father had the opportunity of studying the Customs records for the eighteenth century, from which he copied reports relevant to this stretch of coast. We also discovered one leather-bound accounts ledger, which alone has somehow survived, written in William's own hand. It covers the years 1751-59.

The following account has been concocted from the entries in the ledger and Customs records, with a sprinkling of known historical facts and the help of a vivid imagination! The result is a tantalising glimpse into the roguish duplicity of William Craik's life.

One June evening in 1791 William was hard at work supervising two women planting replacement trees in his avenue. The flies were like a plague of locusts and the two women girned as they dug the holes. William had got the trees from his nephew at Shambellie who had told him that unless he watered them in forthwith and kept them watered "they wouldna do".

They would have to do: he was already eighty-seven summers old and although he felt as fit as ever, his avenue would have to hurry if he was to see it completed. His labours were interrupted by the arrival of a lone horseman who introduced himself most respectfully.

"Mr Craik, I am Robert Burns, Exciseman of Dumfries, come to see you in my own time to see if you will intercede for me wi' my superiors."

William exhorted the women to carry on the good work and asked Burns down to the house. Since it was a matter concerning the Excise, that most admirable body, it must be looked into.

Robert Burns explained that he had recently incurred the wrath of his superiors by purchasing four guns with his own money and gifting them to the French Convention. He went on to say that not

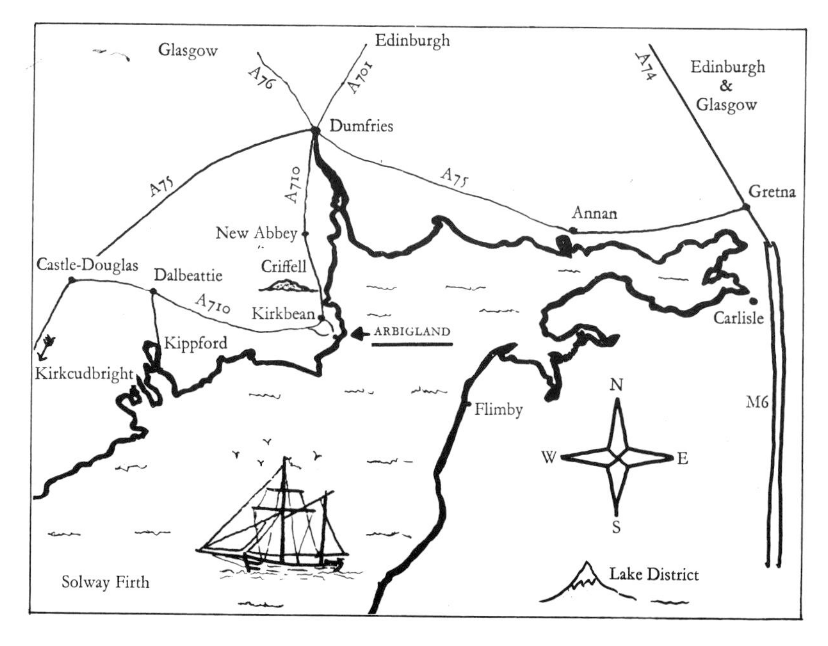

Map of the area

for anything would he displease the Service — had he not an income of £90 a year from it? — it was just that he had a great sympathy with the French working man. He had come, he said, to the one man in the district whom he thought could save him from dismissal; a man who had been a Commissioner of Excise for thirty-three years, a provost of Dumfries, and whose estate was the admiration of southern Scotland.

William did not take long in thought. "I too owe much to the Excise and also admire some French habits, therefore I will write on your behalf. Now be gone as I have work to do." William's admiration extended more to claret than to any Convention; nonetheless he was not unwilling to help his fellow Exciseman.

The women were too busy delving to notice the faraway look on the Laird's face as he bid the poet farewell, or the smile which occasionaly covered it as he thought back across his own dealings with the Excise for the last eighty-odd years. . . .

He remembered how his father and Mr Oswald of Cavens had run cargoes ashore at Arbigland and how he, even as a small boy, had assisted. He recalled the grey dawns spent watching, landward, for the Excise man, the wet nights waiting on the merse.

> Robert Stewart being examined saieth that he, having discovered a small boott hovering along the Cooste . . . did watch him all day . . . Att last the sd little boat cam to the werry creek where he was watching, being about half a mile distant from the dwelling house of the Laird of Arbigland . . . Robert Stewart . . . lay undiscovered to observe what could be done and so soone as the watter fell from about the boat, the crew fell immediately to disload the boat, the said Robert Stewart he went to and boarded her which he seazed with her cargo consisting of twelve runlets containing about ten gallons each . . . the boatmen all went away till about four o'clock in the morning when the boatmen returned with three horses and two servants belonging to the said Laird of Arbigland — no sooner than they cam on board but the two of them laid violentt hands on him and held the said Robert Stewart untill the other third disloaded the cargo — where itt was cleared he could not discover but does suspect that seeing Arbigland's servants and horses were present, it probably may be lodged either in or near his dwelling house . . . We made a diligent search in all the houses and suspected places about and particularly the dwelling house of the Laird of Arbigland when we found two of the Ankers above

mentioned . . . we are heartly sorie that the gentlemen of this Countrie give so much encouragement to those rogues. For if they had not their countenance they would not dare such insults. . . .

from the correspondence book of the Dumfries Excise Officer to his superiors in Edinburgh.

In his mind's eye William saw himself as a grown man, Provost of Dumfries and all of eighteen, and recalled his resolve to improve his inheritance by hard work and thrift. And work hard he did, long years of channelling his energies and resources into improving the Estate of Arbigland. His fortunes were boosted when, at the age of thirty-nine, he became an Exciseman himself.

William Craik, ye are by these presents sworn and deputed Commissioner of Excise twixt foot of Nith and foot of Urr. . . .

It was then that the coffers of Arbigland really began to swell, for his payment was a share of the value of any contraband he confiscated.

June 4 1754: To my 3d. share of 27 Casks spirits seized by me at Saterness 107 Gallns. Rum 74 Dos. Brandy x 40 Gallns. Geniva £16 0s 2d
To Charges on Do. allowed £2 12s 0d
July 19 1754: To my ¼th Share of 2 Holds. Claret 2 half Holds. White wine + 4 doz bottles Do. seized by me & jam. Robinson at Carse £7 2s 11d
To Charges advanced by my more than my share and left by Jam. Robinson in the Coller. hands 16s 3d

Ledger entry made out to John Young Esq., Collector of the Customs, Dumfries. *

Then too did work on his new house begin in earnest. And as fast as the Customs bounty came in, equally rapidly did he spend it — on chimneys, corridors, cornices . . .

Aug 1756: By 34 days at chimney tops and breaking out Air holes in the Walls & setting a Chimney @ 1/1¾... £1 19s 9¼d
Jany. 31 1757: By 29 days to date inclusive at New house & office houses at 10d. £1 4s 2d
July 12 1757: By 85½ days hewing Cornice for

Great Gate in office houses hewing and laying pavement in West Corridor & sundries @ 1/13pn. £4 15s

Ledger entry, marked 'Contra'

By 1765 William's efforts had been rewarded. That year, at haymaking, he sat on his horse in the meadows above the new mansion. William could not help swelling with pride. The house was complete, indeed the lead roof still shone in the sun, not yet weathered. A swarm of little figures like ants were putting the final touches to the stable quadrant. Further afield there crawled, also like ants, other groups of men and women laying out the policies and gardens under the watchful eye of old John Paul, the head gardener, whom he had engaged to create grounds to match the splendour of the new mansion.

William rode on, past the new smiddy which was a hive of activity, four horses waiting to be shod and doubtless two within. It would be a bad thing if it wasna busy — had it not cost him £3.6.0. to build a dozen years before?

After another half mile he paused again, on top of the hill overlooking Tallowquhairn. Laid out before him, like a map, was a project to stir the heart. To the north lay nearly four hundred acres of merse. Ten years earlier, having improved the rest of his land, William had resolved to bring this area into fruitful production. In the first three fields his gaze fell upon a fine stand of barley just beginning to change colour, a level expanse dotted with ricks; in the distance cattle grazed good green grass next to the sea.

The next sixty acres presented a completely different scene. Again the colony of ants sprang to William's mind. There were big ants and little ants, for over fifty horses and more than two hundred men and women were involved. Over forty deep drains perfectly parallel inched towards a deep canal leading to the sea. Some ants even vanished below ground or reappeared from holes as they dug the wells which William had invented to pierce the clay and reach the gravel beneath. William could envisage his projected jigsaw of hedges and ditches spearating fields of oats, barley and grass. It

* Ledger entries show that between June 4 1754 and January 12 1755 he received a total of just over £49 Sterling, a sum which today can be rendered as approximately £24,000, an impressive sum by any standards.

Elizabeth Stewart, sister of Charles Stewart of Shambellie, married William Craik of Arbigland, *William de'Nume, died 1750*

would be a long job and he was already over sixty.

Then in 1772 the collapse of Fordyce's banking house in London brought ruin on many Scottish investors. This was a setback indeed for William, and for other members of the family too. William recalled an unusually cold day in 1775 when, wet and chilled, he broke his journey to call on his nephew, William Stewart of Shambellie. As he approached he noted how well his nephew's mile-long avenue was coming on. The storm-streaked sunset filtered

William Craik of Arbigland (artist unknown). *Photograph Tom Scott*

down through the autumn leaves, many of which had already fallen. William Stewart welcomed his uncle and sent a girl to make tea. The wet coat was spread over a chair before a blazing coal fire and soon steamed itself dry. The two lairds talked mostly of trees, and Craik, who knew how low his nephew's fortunes then stood, made no enquiry as to the origin of the coals, the tea, or the brandy with which it was laced. In these parts at that time it was best not to know how your host came by such pleasant refinements. . . .

After a while he had set out again to ride the last hour home. The rain had stopped and the odd star glimmered weakly between the clouds. William paused soon after passing the Drum and looked down to the Pow. Showers of sparks rose up against the black sky as the workers in his brick and tile works laboured on into the night. To his right he could just make out the square shape of the Brickhouse which the Laird of Cavens had recently completed with bricks bought from William's works. The production there was excellent, but the cost of the coal and the duty thereon made for very slim profits; moreover, he was using almost the entire output of drainage tiles on his own Carse reclamation scheme.

Sometimes William felt he had bitten off more than he could chew when he started on those four hundred acres of cold unyielding clay. He had been at it for twenty years, and only half the Carse had been reclaimed, at a cost of thousands and the lives of two men buried alive when wells collapsed.

After he reached home William sat by his fire and pondered, striking a balance sheet in his head. The estate expenses of the last fifty years had been prodigious: the house alone had cost nigh on four thousand pounds, but his excise bounty had covered much of that. He had recently lost over one thousand pounds in the Fordyce fiasco and since his retiral earlier that year even his excise bounty had ceased.

In addition, the messy business with Dunn the groom had turned out to be an expensive adventure. There had been no need to shoot the man when a good thrashing would have served — and sheriffs were deuced expensive folk to sweeten. Anyway, William, who had a soft spot for the ladies himself, could harldy blame Dunn for falling in love with Helen; he probably would have done so himself if she had not been his daughter. But Adam had taken it as an affront to the family and caused a very tricky and costly few months, but at least the business had been settled. If only his other worries could be resolved so satisfactorily.

William's finances were perilously close to the rocks, that chill autumn day in 1775. Something would have to be done to right the ship.

Although it was approaching midnight, William stirred up the fire, added a few logs, and lay back in his chair. He had two problems to solve. The first was that it was almost impossible to run his tile and brick works profitably with the exorbitant duty on Cumberland coals. This really rankled with him. On a clear day he could see the mines from which the coal came across the water; the coal boats sailed from Maryport and Allonby, which were only a few miles from his other estate at Flimby; moreover, some of the mine owners were his friends. It really was an exasperating situation — and one that could not be resolved legally. The answer, surely, was to run the coal over by night straight into the Carse pow; his mine-owning friends would be happy to accept an extra shilling a ton to despatch the coal without papers. . . .

And indeed the tide *did* turn at the brick and tile factory, although its progress was not always without impediment:

> Honourable Sirs,
>
> . . . receive a Return of seizure of coals made by Paldwain Martine, Tydesman . . . he & a Constable had to watch them all night and about midd night a man with no other cloaths on but a pair of Britches and a large stick in his hand came upon them both unawares and beat them very severely and then made his escape towards CARSETHORN . . .
>
> *from the correspondence book of the Dumfries Excise Officer to his superiors in Edinburgh.*

William's second problem was a simple matter of too little income and too much expenditure. While a Commissioner for Excise he had often earned one hundred pounds each year, which had gone a long way towards paying for his estate improvements, but now all that was finished. The last candle in the room had burned out, but William thought on by the light of the fire. An idea was forming in his mind. . . .

In January the following year William sent his grandson Douglas on a missiont to America. His natural son James, the product of a youthful affair, whom William had always counted as his son, had shown a leaning towards medicine and had taken his chance of fortune in the New World. He had established himself as a successful doctor and prosperous landowner in Port Tobacco, Maryland, whose rich tobacco plantations were proving such a lure to European traders with an eye for a lucrative deal. Surely there was something for William here. No doubt James had an abundance of useful contacts. . . .

Jan. 15th 1776.
My Dear Son,
I send this day by hand of your nephew Douglas whom I trust finds you in good health and prosperous state.
Douglas will explain to you certain matters best not put on paper and I hope you may see some solution to them.
Mistress Craik joins me in sending you our kindest regards.
I remain your affect. father

W.C.

He wanted no obvious connection to be made between Arbigland and far-off Maryland, and he remembered the name of a Scotsman, Coutts, who worked as an agent in Amsterdam, offering various 'factoring' services for merchandise. Coutts was just the sort of man he needed. . . .

William completed his plans by paying a visit to young Douglas at Balcarry, leaving Adam in charge at home. When Douglas returned in the autumn, William's plans were laid and the Balcarry Company of Merchants was formed. Douglas assured his grandfather that, although matters political in the American colonies were far from happy, his Uncle James would arrange things.

It was not long before consignments of good American tobacco — and spirits forbye — began mysteriously to appear in that remote corner of Scotland.

In 1778 a strange coincidence occurred which owed nothing to William's plans but did much to help them. The most dashing and able commander of the American navy, then in its infancy, turned out to be none other than the son of old John Paul the gardener. He had gone off to sea seventeen years before, acquiring at some stage the name of Jones. Now known as Paul Jones, he was terrorising the whole of the British coast to such an extent that the Royal Navy had better things to do than worry about the contents of the holds of passing schooners. The Customs cutters usually ran for home on sighting a larger ship lest it proved to be the dreaded Jones. William was extremely amused. Who would ever have thought that the barefoot boy he had leathered so often for fruit stealing would now prove such an ally to his plans!

He chuckled as he remembered how his passion for symmetry in the house and its gardens had been neatly put in its place by the gardener and his boy. One day, years ago, he had been inspecting the

Arbigland about 1760

walled garden with old John Paul when, glancing up at the window of one of the pair of fruit-houses he saw a terrified face.

"What is that child doing there?" he demanded of the head gardener.

"I caught him stealing fruit, sir."

William glanced up at the other fruit-house and there saw young John's face. "Ha! and your boy was at it too, I see."

"Oh, no sir," replied the gardener, "I just put him there for symmetry."

Yes, John Paul and his family were a smart lot!

By 1779 the tide had turned and things were going very well for William. He celebrated by going to the Grahams of Netherby and buying a highly bred mare to carry him on his frequent — often nocturnal — journeys about the coast. He was well pleased with himself. Who would have thought he could have made such a complete recovery. Not only had he been able to continue his work on the Carse, but he had also made provision for his future estate: the completion in 1776 of the Kirkbean Church — at a cost of £365 8s 1d — would surely assist his passage to the next world. Thank God for spirits and tobacco!

But luck was not always with William. In 1780 Paul Jones moved his attention to France and the Customs cutters became more active again. While William could sweeten the Kirkcubright crew and work with them, he had to appear above reproach to the Carsethorn officer and his men since they were his tenants and any dealings with them would lead to local gossip. Losing his booty could sometimes be safer than challenging the Excise men.

> Honble Sirs,
>
> Information having been sent to us . . . that there had been a considerable landing of smuggled foods at Balcarry we thought it proper to communicate that intelligence to the Collector and Comptroller at Kirkcudbright . . . in consequence of which several parties were sent out from here accompanied by the military. In the meantime the boat crew stationed at Carsethorn had gone round to Balcarry to try if they could seize any of the said goods and they were accordingly so lucky as to find out a concealed cellar in which was thirty-six casks of spirits. . . .
>
> *From the correspondence book of the Dumfries Excise Officer to his superiors in Edinburgh, 22 September 1780.*

In 1782, at seventy-nine years of age, William had begun to slow down. Most of his projects were nearing completion and many were bearing fruit in the form of increased rents and turning into profit where he farmed himself. He had steered the ship clear of the rocks and redeemed almost all his bonds. Then fortune dealt a cruel blow. One wild day Adam was at sea arranging for the delivery of a cargo when he was surprised by a Customs cutter. In the chase that followed, Adam's yacht capsized and all hands were lost.

The smile that had played across William's lips faded. Yes indeed, he owed much to the Excise; through them he had had many adventures which had brought him fortune but had also taken his son's life. After Adam's death he had wound down his Merchants' Company and retired from "the trade". In any case the Prime Minister, Mr Pitt, had more or less put paid to the game with his Commutation Act. William had settled to spend the last years of his life quietly making inexpensive improvements to his property — like the new trees he was planting that very day. He thought again of Robert Burns's plea to intercede on his behalf with the Excise, and set off to the house to take up pen and paper.

William Craik himself designed the new house at Arbigland; largely unaltered, it remains a worthy monument to a remarkable man.

But Craik was not the only one whose spirit is still felt at Arbigland. A ghostly horseman is known to ride by the main gates; it is said to be Dunn the ill-fated groom, still haunting the childhood home of his beloved Helen.

Helen, a renowned poetess, left Arbigland in 1792 never to return. The opening stanza of her melancholy "Lines Written in the Summerhouse at Arbigland in 1792" were written in that same year and convey clearly the cry of this broken-hearted woman:

> *Derived of peace — to calumny a prey,*
> *Here Helen wept her lonely hours away;*
> *Though guiltless, forc'd imputed guilt to bear,*
> *No justice destin'd — and no pity near.*

Dr James Craik, William's illegitimate son, had a happier fate. His fortunes flourished and he enjoyed great prominence as a physician and pioneer in America's medical profession. He became George Washington's doctor — and close friend — and was at his bedside when the great President died.

Although Dr James survived his father, he was unable to inherit Arbigland on account of his birth. The estate passed to a cousin from whose son my ancestor bought Arbigland in 1852.

Ardchattan Priory

Alastair Lorne Campbell

ARDCHATTAN

Ardchattan is situated some six miles from Connel on the north bank of Loch Etive, that Highland fiord that pierces far into the mountains of Argyll from its mouth at the tidal cataract of the Falls of Lora. It is wild country, this, but the Priory itself is well sheltered between the two promontories that flank a bay, looking almost due south across the waters of the loch to the hills of Lorn beyond. A luxuriant shrubbery and tall trees shield the house from the prevailing west wind, while a high garden wall and the ruins of the old chapel take the edge off the infrequent but piercing east wind. To landward, a cluster of outbuildings, cottages and farm steadings cling to the houses; to seaward, a sweep of lawn flanked by flower-beds rolls right down to the low wall hiding the narrow road which follows the line of the shore. Even with the vagaries of the Argyllshire weather, it is almost impossible to think of Ardchattan without an overall impression of sunlight and peace, the peace that comes so often with old places.

And Ardchattan is very old indeed. The present Laird is Colonel Robert Campbell-Preston, Her Majesty's Vice-Lieutenant for the County of Argyll, whose family have been at Ardchattan for four hundred years. Time enough, but Ardchattan goes back another two hundred and fifty years earlier to its foundation in 1231. This, it is said, makes it the second-oldest continuously inhabited house in Scotland.

Such a house cannot fail to have a story and I have long been interested in the tale that Ardchattan has to tell. Perhaps I have a deeper interest than in my earlier days when I was roped in to show parties round the house when it was opened to visitors. This was a by no means unpleasing task, provided you always remembered to shut the intervening doors between the various rooms so that your party could not hear the guide next door telling a completely different version of your last story. I remember being in particularly fine form on one occasion when, on completing the tour, one visitor was kind enough to thank me for my efforts adding that he had learnt of various aspects of Highland history hitherto unknown to him. "Oh, are you interested in the subject, then?" said I with the magnificent condescension of extreme youth. "Well, yes I am," was the devastating reply, "you see I hold the Chair of Scottish History at —" and he named a famous university.

But you can hardly escape history at a place like Ardchattan. The modern wallpaper suddenly gives way to stonework that is seven hundred and fifty years old, while outside in the garden, a shallow dip marks the site of a pond where for hundreds of years the monks came for their Friday fish. There are surprises, too. Some years ago there was a near panic when the building of the new kitchen unearthed a seven-foot-tall skeleton in the old wall. Any alteration carried out here is bound to reveal traces of the distant past although few, thank goodness, are as gruesome as that one.

It is not easy to know where to start the story. The location of Ardchattan as a site of worship goes back even beyond the arrival of the monks that were the first occupants of the priory. A few hundred yards away, up the hill, is an old ruined chapel, apparently the latest of a number of primitive churches that succeeded each other here. It is dedicated to St Baodan, a long-forgotten early Celtic saint who appears to have had his cell here. These early missionaries very often built on the sites of worship of the pagan religion they wished to supplant; the transfer of loyalty was made that much easier if the location remained unchanged. The ancient Celtic races were worshippers of rock and water; it is surely more than coincidence that a few yards away, made respectable by the name "Tobar Baodan" — "St Baodan's Wall" — is a spring now deep in a thicket of laurel that still has the local reputation of granting the wishes of its votaries. I can only say that at three moments of crisis in my life I have flung a coin into its dark depths and have muttered a wish. I have yet to be disappointed. Another object of pagan veneration no doubt was the vast boulder that stood a mile or so to the east, in Glen Sallach. Translated from the Gaelic as "the Seat of Baodan", it was an object of veneration for countless generations until, during the last century, an east coast builder with more Saxon blood than Celtic in his veins, split the stone and carted the pieces down the hill and along the shore to Ardchattan where he made them into the gate pillars that guard the entrance into the chapel burying-ground.

The first sure date is 1193, when, in a sunny valley in far-off Burgundy the Holy Viardus founded the Order of Monks that were to become known because of their first home in Val-des-Choux as the Valliscaulian Order, or the "Kail Glen Monks". Some forty years later the Order was ready to expand overseas and their offer to come to Scotland was well received by a King who saw the establishment of religious houses in the land as an aid to bringing stability to the country. The Valliscaulians set up three priories in what were then the furthest reaches of the King's Writ. Besides Ardchattan, there was Beauly Priory and as the headquarters of the Order in Scotland, the Priory of Pluscarden in Moray. Each needed the support of a local potentate to become established: in men, in money, in material and in protection. Ardchattan's founder was Duncan MacDougall "de Ergadia" — of Argyll — the mighty Lord of Lorn.

Duncan was a grandson of Somerled, the seafaring King of Argyll and the Isles. His first cousin was Donald from whom sprang the Lords of the Isles and the powerful clan that took their name of Macdonald from him. For generations, these Lords of the Isles played off their allegiance between the King of Scotland and the King of Norway, thereby managing to rule largely independently of both; Dougal, the father of Duncan, was given a portion that included much of mainland Argyll and his interest was therefore best served by placating the King of Scots. The foundation of Ardchattan was also an insurance policy for his future welfare in the next world while he also safeguarded his position in this one by building the powerful fortress of Dunstaffnage which overlooks the Sound of Mull from the entrance to Loch Etive.

The Valliscaulian Order was a strict one: of the Cistercian persuasion, it nevertheless had overtones of the Carthusian Rule to which Viardus, the founder, had himself originally belonged. The monks at Ardchattan wore hair-shirts under their robes which were white in colour. They ate no meat and they observed a vow of silence, performing various religious offices alone, although they came together for worship in the chapel, they ate together in the refectory and they slept in a dormitory. Otherwise, they spent long hours each labouring assiduously in his own little enclosure; the flat pasture between the house and the hill was for many centuries known as "the Monks' Garden".

They began by building the Chapel, now a roofless ruin; then, to the west of it, the rectangular Cloister, with, on the south side, the conventional buildings that form the underlying fabrics of the house today. It seems likely that there were no major buildings round the other sides of the cloister, although no doubt a cluster of huts would have sheltered close to this as do the present cottages and outbuildings on that side of the house. As the mansion has grown, it has swallowed the old cloister and has filled it up and overflowed beyond, but it is still possible, here and there, to find a cross carved in the stone of what was once the cloister's outer wall. With its conglomeration of little flats and cottages, Ardchattan has still quite a population of humans, dogs, cats and hens; there is still a cheerful clatter about the place and the lowing of cattle at milking time, very much, one imagines, as has been the case these three-quarters of a thousand years past.

For the monks the powerful protection of the Lords of Lorn was

The Abbey in ruins, *Royal Commission on Ancient Monuments, Scotland*

probably even more efficacious than the stone crosses that are said to have marked the boundaries of the priory and to have given sanctuary to all those that sought it within their confines. "Happy is the Land that has no History", and there is little to relate of Ardchattan's early years. But at the end of the thirteenth century even remote Ardchattan found itself involved in the war for Scotland's independence.

In 1296, Peter, Prior of Ardchattan, along with his fellow dignataries of the Church, had to go off and sign the Act of Homage to Edward of England. This may not have been as distasteful as it might seem. The MacDougalls were no supporters of the Bruce who had murdered the Lord of Lorn's brother-in-law Comyn; they were on the side of Baliol and his English friends and helped him at every turn. So it was that in 1308, Robert the Bruce, now firmly on the throne, turned his attention to his ancient foes in the west and came looking for them with an army. The obvious place to stop his advance was in the Pass of Brander across the loch from Ardchattan, where the River Awe on its short journey between Loch Awe and the sea, foams through a narrow defile under the precipitous flanks of Ben Cruachan. Here on the narrow path, a few men could hold an army, and indeed would have done had not Douglas — "the Good Sir James" — led a flanking party up and over a shoulder of the mountain. This came down like an avalanche upon the Men of Lorn who broke and fled across the Awe. Bruce and his men went after them and cut them down without mercy; the stone cairns that mark their graves are still to be seen today in a meadow by the riverside.

On swept the King and came to Dunstaffnage, chief stronghold of his enemies. The castle fell after a short siege and in it he installed a garrison under a Campbell Constable, a member of that family from whom he had received much help and whose rise to a power that was to dominate the West Highlands dates from this epoch.

When the fighting was done, it appears that King Robert made his headquarters at Ardchattan, for it was here a week or two later that he summoned what has been described as "the Last Gaelic Parliament". This is certainly a misnomer; it was most likely an assembly of the local warlords, summoned to Ardchattan by land and sea so that they might be in no doubt whatsoever of the King's wishes. They met in the monks' refectory — sitll the dining room of today's house — where you may stand and look out on the sparkling waters of the loch as they did while listening to the harsh Norman

French of the King, followed by the sibilant Gaelic of the interrpeter.

But Ardchattan seems to have prospered in spite of its troubled surroundings. As early as 1274, when the Tax Roll was compiled (known by its author's name today as "Bagimond's Roll") Ardchattan is shown with a value of £200 yearly as opposed to the Bishopric of Argyll whose vastly larger extent is rated at no more than £293. As well as the priory lands and the income of the neighbouring Kilbadon Church, the monks were supported by the income from several West Highland churches which included Kilmonivaig in Lochaber, Kirkapol in Tiree and Kilmarow in Kintyre. A later charter shows that they owned the salmon netting at the mouth of the River Awe and at the head of Loch Etive as well as a tenth share of all the salmon and herring caught from one end of the loch to the other. All this for a commmunity which by its own regulations could not exceed twenty in number, lay brothers included.

As with the church as a whole, such fat living led inevitably to luxury and decline. It wasn't just over-indulgence at table, either. As early as 1411, we have the Papal Letter appointing Christinus MacDonald, monk of Ardchattan, to be Prior of Beauly in place of Prior Matthew who, regrettably, is described as "a notorious fornicator"!

One of the more lurid stories told on the "Grand Tour" of Ardchattan has always been recounted in what is known as the "Prior's Room" — the panelled study to the east of the old refectory/dining room where the prior is said to have had his quarters. It concerns a prior of Ardchattan who indulged in similar malpractices with a nun from the nunnery at Kilmaronaig across the water. They lived together to the general scandal which reached as far afield as the Order's Scottish headquarters at Pluscarden, far to the north. A surprise visit of inspection caught out the couple; there was only just time for the Prior to hide his inamorata in a recess under the floor of his room with the muttered promise that she would be released as soon as the unwelcome visitor could be speeded on his way. Unfortunately the visit lasted a fortnight, during which time the guest of honour had to be given lodging in his brother Prior's quarters; there was no opportunity for the girl to escape and the story goes that she is there still.

The Prior's room, below which the nun was hidden and entombed, *Royal Commission on Ancient Monuments, Scotland*

Just a good story? Well, as it happens, in the lower ground floor beneath where a hypocaust gave some heat at least to the monks, there is an inexplicable but apparently solid block of masonry, several metres square, for no apparent reason. and, quite recently, the record has been found of an order given in 1506 by Prior James of Pluscarden to his colleague at Beauly to visit Ardchattan forthwith and there "make such regulation as he should find necessary". Finally, a charter dated some thirty years later, reveals that there was indeed a change of Prior at Ardchattan around this time.

By the end of the sixteenth century, the church was in considerable decline. In the case of such establishments as Ardchattan this was largely due to the care of "Commendators" — often laymen, who were put in charge and were tacitly allowed to divert its revenues to their own pockets.

In 1573, the Commendator of Ardchattan was one John Campbell, Bishop of the Isles, a grandson of the Earl of Argyll who fell with his King on Flodden Field, and offspring of the stormy union between the Earl's third son, also John, with Muriel, the heiress of Cawdor, in Nairn. Her ward and marriage having been secured by Argyll, a party under Campbell of Inverliver was sent off to the north, to bring back this valuable prize, who was still only a young child. Muriel was handed over all right, but not before her nurse, for future identification, had bitten off the top joint of her little finger. Someone remarked to Inverliver that the Campbells had not yet gained Cawdor; to do so, Muriel must live long enough to produce a Campbell heir. To this, Inverliver is said to have replied, "Muriel can never die while there is a red-haired lassie on the banks of Loch Awe . . ." and no doubt a missing finger joint would have presented but a little problem if a substitute had to be found! But it was a far cry to Loch Awe and long before they got there a much larger force led by Muriel's uncles caught up with them. Inverliver left his sons in a circle surrounding an upturned basket which the Cawdors duly believed to cover the child, and with his precious burden Inverliver slipped away through the hills. He never saw his sons again. Muriel, however, survived, married happily and the fat acres of Cawdor passed to the Campbells.

John was one of the results of this story, and with him Ardchattan passed into the hands of the family that own it today. It was actually an illegitimate son that he chose to succeed him as Prior. Alexander was probably chosen as having the best chance of keeping the property in family hands. He was later legitimised and in 1602 received a Royal Charter of Ardchattan which is still among the family papers. There seems to have been some deal struck with the head of the Campbells of Cawdor who retained the right to visit the priory whenever and for as long as he with his whole family wished and there be entertained; furthermore, he could call on Campbell of Ardchattan to look after and bring up any of his children up to the age of ten. So far, no Earl Cawdor has put this requirement to the test!

Alexander's marriage was a somewhat strange one, albeit extremely fortunate as later events were to prove. His wife was a daughter of the Earl of Antrim and therefore an Irish Macdonald. A generation later, their son John was to bless this connection when, during the Civil Wars, Argyll was invaded by Montrose's army, a savage crew of Irish, and men of the Isles. Their commander was Alasdair MacColla, often given his father's name of Colkitto Macdonald, and third cousin to the Prior. This lucky link ensured that Ardchattan was spared the ravages inflicted so devastatingly upon most of the Campbell lands. When the motley crowd of ruffians eventually drew off to the north, Alexander provided boats for them to cross the loch at Connel, as glad to see the back of his cousin's troops as they were to avoid the long trudge round the head of the loch. Behind them they left a wide swathe of destruction, blackened rafters and the crying of children; with them they took great herds of plundered cattle which they drove into the sea, to swim across the narrow mouth of the loch. The tide was ebbing fast and many of the cattle were swept down over the Falls of Lora. Some of them came ashore at Dunstaffnage and were rescued but most were swept out to sea and drowned.

In passing it is worth commenting here on the propensity of Campbells to marry other Campbells; I did myself and my father before me. It is not, as some people have been unkind enough to claim, that no one else will touch us: rather, that we know a good thing when we see it! John's mother came of a family long at enmity with our clan; after the Macdonalds, the people that did the most damage to us were undoubtedly the men of Atholl. It is of considerable historical irony that the present Laird of Ardchattan is stepfather to the Duke of Atholl. Colonel Campbell-Preston's late wife was the Hon. Angela Pearson, sister of Lord Cowdray. Her first husband was Lt-Colonel Tony Murray who would have succeeded to the Dukedom of Atholl had he not been killed in action commanding the Scottish Horse, the regiment which her second husband was also to command and in which he won a well-earned Military Cross. Angela Campbell-Preston had a remarkable talent as an architect although she never trained formally as such. Both in Argyll and in Atholl some eighty houses, flats and cottages owe their comfort to her efforts in building and adapting. She did much to improve Ardchattan and it is she that is responsible for the lightwell that illuminates the centre of the house with its first floor wrought-iron balustrade displaying the Campbell swan, the Preston unicorn and the demi-gryphon of the Cowdrays. She was much loved and respected both in Argyll and in Atholl, those two areas long at enmity with each other and when she died, the churches in both were packed with those from all walks of local life who wanted to be there.

But if that first fortune in marriage spared Ardchattan, it was not for long. The Laird of Ardchattan was involved in Glencairn's Rising in 1653; the following year, a passage in a report from the Cromwellian Colonel Lilburne to the GOC Scotland contains the following:

> "Nor was Captain Mutloe in the Westerne Highlands idle, for hearing that the Laird Archatan (being one of the Chief

> Malignants in Lorne) had garrison'd his house for the Enemy, he drew forth a partie out of Dunstaffnage and Dunolly, fell upon the house, and after some dispute having kill'd 3 of the Enemy, entred the house, and tooke a Lieutenant with some prisoners, and store of armes and ammunition. . . ."

The soldiers stripped the house and fired it; they left the chapel with its ornaments smashed and open to the sky. It was never again restored as a place of worship and it became a burial ground. The house was restored in time, but if today you climb the stairs to the attic, you will find the great roof-beams of the old Priory still blackened and charred by the flames of three centuries ago.

The '45 Rebellion found young Patrick of Ardchattan, son of the house, off to the wars as an officer in the Argyll Militia on the side of the Government against the Jacobite rebels. Patrick soon gained the approbation of his fellows; my ancestor Donald Campbell of Airds writing approvingly of him in 1746: "Petter Ardchattan . . . was so allert that he is become a favourite . . . he is now a compleat hussar . . .". A month later the news was not so good; poor Petter was among a party of sleeping Campbells surprised at Keith by an enemy fighting patrol. Several officers were wounded and the whole party was captured, among them young Patrick who was among those shipped off to France to serve as a bargaining counter in the exchange of Jacobite prisoners held by the Government. He was lucky, however, by comparison with my late father-in-law, another Patrick, whom I have already mentioned. *His* captivity started at St Valery in 1940 and lasted five full weary years ending up, after three valiant escapes, in the notorious castle of Colditz.

Not long after Culloden, Ardchattan was again touched by drama. The Laird's brother-in-law, Colin Campbell of Glenure, was shot in the back as he rode homeward through Appin having been carrying out his duties as Crown Factor for the forfeited estates of Callart and Ardshield. His appalled companions just caught a glimpse of his killers as they scrambled away up the steep hillside.

The Government reacted promptly — over-reacted, many would claim. They were very much on edge, fearing another attempt by the Pretender in the West Highlands. After collecting the evidence, what there was of it, they arrested the luckless James Stewart — "James of the Glen" — for complicity in the crime. He was tried at Inveraray by a jury largely composed of local Campbell lairds, found guilty and duly taken to Ballachulish where he was hanged. Today's motorway sweeps you past the monument on a hillock overlooking the straits where his bones were chained together on the gibbet so that they might long serve as an awful warning to those who incurred the Government's wrath. The true murderer was never identified. His name is said to be known to various local families whose heirs on coming of age have the secret passed on to them, generation after generation. Among the prime suspects has long been a rather unsavoury figure, one Alan "Breck" Stewart, so called from the traces of smallpox that disfigured his face, who was in the area on a surreptitious recruiting for the French army in which he served. Robert Louis Stevenson in *Kidnapped* has made a hero of him and has denigrated poor Colin with the title of "the Red Fox", a name he never had in real life. It was to Ardchattan that his body was carried and it lies under a stone slab in the chapel, alongside his relations of the Barcaldine family to which he belonged.

In 1787, Patrick of Ardchattan's son, Alexander, was on a tour on the Continent. His letter home recounts how, one day in Paris, "a tall, ugly man" came to see him, saying that he was from Appin and had wrongly been accused of the murder of Alexander's uncle . . ."I was not a little surprised with such an introduction and wished to get rid of him as soon as possible, he denied the murder and swore by all that was sacred it was not him, that he knew who it was but was bound by oath to conceal it, but that the world would know it after his death by his papers. . . ." the letter is at Ardchattan on display, but Alan Breck's papers seem to have died with him or someone took pains to see they never revealed the true name of the murderer.

The story still rouses passion today. As it happens it would appear that the unhappy James Stewart was indeed guilty as charged, of being "Art and Part" of the murder; it is inconceivable that he did did not know of what was afoot. The spot where the crime took place is off the road to Oban from Ballachulish, where a modern cairn with an inscription marks the spot. Colonel Campbell-Preston was one of the joint instigators of its erection which nearly never took place. His partner in the scheme was a distinguished Stewart laird; he wanted the wording to read "where Colin Campbell of Glenure was *killed*— Ardchattan insisted on, and eventually got the inscription, "was murdered".

The Campbells of Barcaldine are not the only family to have used the burial-ground in the chapel. Nearby, in a special aisle, lie the

Campbells of Lochnell who, four hundred and fifty years after they branched off the main stem of the Earls of Argyll, are still next in line to the Dukedom of Argyll should that family fail. The Campbells of Inverawe are there and, of course, the Campbells of Ardchattan themselves. The old chapel also houses a magnificent carved tomb of two mediaeval Macdougall priors and their family. Next to it is the gravestone of Mackintyre of Glen Noe, Chief of his name, which displays the white hat in winter and the snowball in summer, the rent by which he held his lonely glen, further up the loch below the corries of Cruachan. The seventeenth- and eighteenth-century tombs display as emblems of mortality the skull and crossbones as was the fashion of the day; this calls forth ribald and unjustified comment from English tourists who profess to have their views on the piratical antecedents of the Oban trades-people thus confirmed. This used to be the burial place of the Magdougall chief until, in the eighteenth century, a fierce storm prevented the funeral cortege of the then chief from making the crossing. After three days, his bearers turned away and trudged through the hills to Kilbride, thenceforth the burial ground of the former Lords of Lorn. "Carsewell's weather" is still the local term for these storms; a name which dates back four hundred years and more to the death, in 1573, of John Carsewell, Bishop of the Isles, who was the producer of the

Sketch of Ardchattan by the author

first book in Gaelic; a translation of John Knox's Liturgy. The barge carrying his coffin broke loose in the storm and vanished in the spray. Three days later it was cast ashore on the point which goes by his name a few hundred yards from Ardchattan and he, too, now lies within its walls.

The male line of the Campbells of Ardchattan died out with "Petter" Ardchattan's grandson, Alexander Glynn Campbell. His sister Jane, Mrs Popham, daughter-in-law of one of Nelson's captains, died childless in 1878 and the property passed to Robert, father of the present laird who was still a schoolboy when he inherited. He descended from "Petter's" daughter, Anne, who in 1777 married the Fifeshire laird, Andrew Clarke of Comrie. This concentrated, if complicated geneaology explains the wide range of family names represented among the portraits on the walls of the house. Robert Clarke-Campbell-Preston, as he became, did not at first want to leave the family home at Valleyfield and it is said, even tried to find a male Campbell heir who might have prior claim to Ardchattan. There was none, and needless to say Ardchattan soon exercised its magical spell on him as on so many others.

Ardchattan is not a *grand* house in any sense, but it is a comfortable and very friendly one. No ghosts roam here, in spite of poor Colin of Glenure's violent end; the many bones that it shelters sleep peacefully without waking. Above all, it is a welcoming house, perhaps the more so because of its remoteness and the wild grandeur of its surroundings. The solitary road up the lochside is still a narrow one, the scene of many a hair-raising encounter round its sharp corners; it does not encourage the casual tourist. In the not-so-old-days, the usual arrival was by boat, rowed across the uncertain waters of Loch Etive from the littered railway station at Achnacloich on the other side. Here it was that my mother-in-law arrived to meet her future in-laws in a train that was far too long for the little platform. London born and bred, she was scarcely prepared for the stentorian bellow of "Jump, girl!" which caused her to fall off of five feet with a bone-jarring thud onto the cinders below. Her mother-in-law had arrived in the same fashion as a new bride at the beginning of this century.

It was at Ardchattan where I actually met my wife for the first time. I was six, and she was all of four. I remember it well or, to be more accurate, I remember the pedal-car in the nursery. This represented the summit of my then earthly ambitions; she represented the chief threat to my possession of it. It was a considerable number of years later, and in spite of the pedal-car, that we were married. As I lay down my pen our anniversary is only a few days away. On or about the due date, I hope to be once more at Ardchattan, to experience again that extraordinarily welcoming sense of benign peace that the old house has brought to so many people over the years.

The Sundial

Earl Haig

BEMERSYDE

The stage coach from the south had reached Galashiels. Not far away at Abbotsford, Sir Walter Scott was ready to welcome his guest, the great painter Joseph Mallord Turner. He had invited Turner to the border country to make some landscape drawings to illustrate an edition of his poetical works. With Scott was Thomas Cadell, the publisher, upon whose advice the invitation had been issued to "take various drawings of remarkable corners and towns and stick them all together". The invitation, wrote Scott, involved "furnishing to the poetical works two decorations to each of the proposed twelve volumes, to wit a print and a vignette to each at the rate of £25 for each, which is cheap enough considering these are the finest specimens of art going".

On the evening of Turner's arrival, Thursday 4th August 1831, Scott was tired and unwell. But his bearing had the serenity of a writer detached from the practical and financial problems which beset him. The cause of the tense expression on his face was anxiety about Turner's visit. He remembered an unhappy experience over a previous joint publication which had resulted in financial loss to both of them. According to him, Turner was "almost the only man of genius I ever knew who is sordid in these matters" and, according to contemporary painter friends like the Reverend John Thomson of Duddingston, Turner was ungenerous about showing his work to fellow painters for fear of disclosing some of his working methods. Happily these doubts were soon dispelled when the painter arrived off the coach, extremely hungry but alert and stimulated by the prospect of making the most of an opportunity which destiny had offered him.

Next morning the painter discussed plans for the excursions with

Scott and Cadell; plans which were to involve four days of marathon driving and walking. Cadell saw to the provision of an umbrella in case of storms and the rowing of boats across the Tweed. These aids came in useful that very day, the first day of the tour, which involved a visit to Walter Scott's original home in the Borders — Ashiestiel. There was a heavy rainstorm whilst Turner was sketching, and a held umbrella was necessary. In order to have a view of the house against the hill a boat was also needed to cross the Tweed.

Owing to the weather and to Scott's frailty, they decided to return home before three o'clock. After dinner Turner had a good talk with Cadell on the subject of Thomas the Rhymer and his prophecy about Bemersyde and of the ballad *The Eve of St John* which had happened at Smailholm. Both these places he would visit the next day.

That day, a Saturday and the second day of the visit, began with wet and fog, but the weather cleared and the party duly set off about 11.30 in the Scott family sociable, a "barouche landau built in London which from the time she [his wife] got it she was seldom out of". Having crossed over the Tweed bridge above Melrose and stopping at a viewpoint near Gattonside, opposite Melrose, they drove on fast to Smailholm Tower, which they reached just before two o'clock. After a quick lunch Turner made some sketches of the tower which was silhouetted on a rocky landscape reflected amongst the reeds and rushes of the loch. Later when Scott was shown the sketches of Smailholm he was delighted with them. It was a place which had a special meaning for him since his childhood days when smitten with infantile paralysis. He had been sent to stay with his uncle, a previous farmer of Sandyknowe, for good food and country air. So it was there that his love for the Borders began. He was pleased with the way Turner had interpreted the Tower and the loch and he realised how completely the artist had understood its character; how he had responded to its peace and isolation and ruggedness. Scott's judgement was proved right when the final illustration was made for *The Eve of St John*. For his part, the gruff old Turner had come face to face with a subject to whose loneliness he could respond, and he must have been pleased to realise that Scott and he really had something in common. Having finished the sketches, Turner was desperate to move on, but departure was delayed because of the warmth of the welcome accorded by the farmer's wife in Sandyknowe farmhouse. Scott found it difficult to tear himself away from the old home, from which he had attended Kelso school. All this involved sitting round for a second lunch in the farmhouse kitchen. It was already four o'clock before they set off for Bemersyde, which they reached shortly after five.

To Turner's relief, the Laird, James Zurrubabel Haig, and his wife were away, so he could concentrate on his work whilst his companions were given a tour of the garden by "the bonny Mary Haig", one of the three daughters of the house. Turner made two sketches, one of the house and the old Spanish chestnut tree, and the second of the sundial. According to Cadell, Turner was not enthusiastic about the appearance of the house and his studies only took half an hour to complete.

The watercolour of Bemersyde which he made from these brief studies was the most profound of all the illustrations for the *Poetical Works*. Its purpose was to illustrate *Sir Tristram*, a poem about a

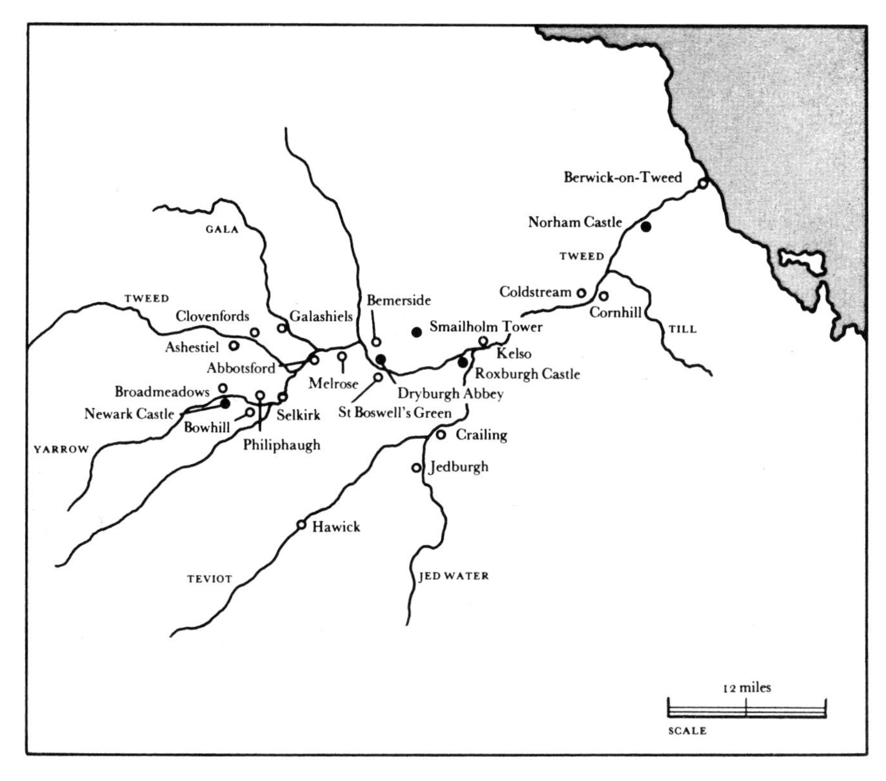

Map from *Landscapes of Memory* by Gerald Finley showing Turner's visit to Abbotsford and Berwick-on Tweed in 1831

Border knight, said to have been written by the thirteenth-century Laird of Ercildoune, Thomas Learmont — better known as "Thomas the Rhymner". According to legend, Thomas went off with the Fairy Queen into Fairyland, in the heart of the Eildons, where he spent seven years acquiring the ability to make prophecies. In one of his prophecies the Rhymer predicted the long future of the Haig family:

Tyde what may
Whate'er betyde
Haig shall be Haig
of Bemersyde.

This prophecy was part of the Borders legendary which Turner had been asked to illustrate. At the centre of the watercolour stands the sundial, put there by Antony Haig in 1690. Like a ticking clock, the shadows on the sundial mark the passing of time, and in his work Turner suggests the long-evolving history of the Haig family at Bemersyde; its past, its present, and its future. In the foreground a parchment volume inscribed with the name "Thomas the Rhymer" is linked with a portrait of an old man whose features have a suggestion of James Zerrubabel, the laird. One hypothesis is that the portrait symbolises old age in contrast to the portrait of young Mary Haig and her kitten playing with balls of wool beside her. The theme, therefore, is that of the passing of time, and the long and evolving history of the Haigs at Bemersyde, dating from the Norman baron, Petrus de Haga, whose name appears on a charter at Bemersyde, written in 1162.

Attention is focused upon the three main figures in the composition. Scott, already frail, is leaning on the arm of his publisher Cadell, with Mary Haig beside them. Time was running out for Scott, and the broken crock with its escaping contents must refer to the imminence of his death.

Time once there was alas but now
that time returns not new again
the shades upon the dial cast
proceed but pass not back again.

Turner has stressed the meaningfulness of art by placing a guitar and a laurel wreath on the sundial to represent the vocation of the creative artist. He himself has withdrawn from the collective scene in the foreground to a life devoted to communion with nature. It is from the great Spanish chestnut tree that he draws his inspiration, and the theme of natural growth is symbolised by the image of flowerpots in the foreground.

Perhaps I should explain that the garden itself has been largely invented — and in a way which no laird of Bemersyde would approve. There was in fact no sunken garden in existence in 1831 although my father later copied the idea and placed a sunken garden very close to where Turner put his. Turner realised that although he had found Bemersyde unsatisfactory as a subject because of the setting of the house, a serious rendering of it was needed. Built as it was in 1535 on top of a hill in a strategic position above the River Tweed to guard the Monksford below, it is out of relationship with the landscape which surrounds it. That landscape is hidden over the brow, and at the time of Turner's visit the problem was accentuated by the garden wall which then existed at the south-west corner of the house, barring a view of the Eildon Hills beyond.

Turner moved the sundial from its situation on the lawn near the back of the picture to the centre of the composition, into the middle of a baroque sunken garden which has urns, out of keeping with the austere fortified tower behind. The medieval knot garden, which my father designed later, has suited the architecture of the house much better. Across the classical garden which Turner created in his mind he allowed the evening light to flow over the house up into the trees and clouds beyond, in the manner of the Dutch. He conveyed the essential character and atmosphere of the house and its environment with extraordinary understanding, but he preferred to romanticise the proportions of the tower in keeping with the mood of Scott's work and there is no reference to the gnarled old hulk of a tree, some six or seven hundred years old at that time, which incidentally had been used as a hanging tree and later as a place to greet friends under. He described it more accurately in the preparatory topographical drawing which is now in the British Museum. However, the artistic vision transcends topography, and Turner's interpretation was in the great classical tradition of Rubens and Claude Lorrain.

But why has he put such strange windows in the peel tower? In his topographical sketch the windows of the second-floor room are shown opened from the bottom so that the lower sections reveal the darkness of the room inside. These darknesses are given a brief stab

Bemersyde Tower, *an engraving by Turner*

Sketch of Bemersyde, *Turner*

with a soft pencil, indications which appear like dark pupils in two frightened eyes. Unfortunately, in the process of transfer from the sketch to the watercolour to the print, these grotesque blacknesses have been given greater emphasis so that the house assumes at that point a touch of surrealism. Perhaps this treatment is due to the need for a focal point. The two black squares of the window apertures are repetitions of the black portrait formed in the foreground and the dark forms leading through the shadows around the sundial up the steps towards the two dark carriage horses. They form the two final full stops in a sequence of six different black forms which recede into space. Perhaps, unconsciously, Turner, who was deeply involved in Venice at that time, gave to the tower a Byzantine touch so that the square, dark apertures of the windows have the appearance of some of the windows on the facade of St Mark's. This hint of the Venetian is echoed by the shape of the sociable, which is not unlike a gondola awaiting its passengers outside a palazzo on the Grand Canal.

Turner could not resist a hint of the Scottish baronial style, which he felt was part of the stage setting of a Borders laird, exemplified at Abbotsford. The rounded archway at the right-hand corner of the house has been correctly observed in the drawing, but is altered to the Gothic style in the final print. The four windows and the small round aperture above, which Turner inserted into his sketch at the east wing, never existed. The idea of a round aperture at that point was suggested to Turner by ones of a similar size which did, and indeed do still exist in the wall which extends out of the picture to the right. Having indicated some of the variations which Turner has introduced into the design of the house, I would add that it is impossible to give adequate praise to the truth of the description of Bemersyde which Turner managed to make from a sketch which had been drawn within the space of half an hour.

When Turner was finished, the three men climbed into the carriage and set off for Abbotsford. Their road took them over Bemersyde Hill, past Sir Walter's favourite view, which they stopped to enjoy and which impressed Turner deeply "with the sun in the direction it now shone in". From that viewpoint they could see the great horseshoe bend of the river, with Old Melrose on the far bank and the Eildon Hills beyond. Scott's thoughts returned to the Rhymer, and his eye was carried on across to the foot of the Eildons to the point of the Eildon Tree near the Boglie Burn where Thomas the Rhymer is believed to have sat when the Fairy Queen came along.

True Thomas lay on Huntlie bank;
A ferlie he spied wi' his ee;
And there he saw a ladye bright,
Come riding down by the Eildon Tree.

According to the legend, Thomas lay for a while on Huntlie bank with the beautiful Fairy Queeen, and of course they fell in love. Without much encouragement, the Rhymer then went off with the Fairy Queen into Fairyland, in the heart of the Eildons, where he spent seven years of blissful happiness. At the end of that time, with great reluctance, he decided to return home. The fairies were angry and began to taunt him but his mind was made up so they rather mockingly bade him farewell.

Upon his return home, Thomas found it hard to accustom himself to the realities of life and for a while he was not recognised and was treated as neither fowl nor fish nor good red herring. However, he gradually resumed his relationships with friends and neighbours, and finally with the king himself, who began to rely on him for advice after the fulfilment of several prophecies. One of these foresaw the extinction of his own name and lairdship of Ercildoune:

"The hare sall kittle [litter] on my hearth-stane,
and there will never be a laird Learmont again."

This prophecy about the fate of his own lineage was in strong contrast to that of the Haigs of Bemersyde. After a while Thomas disappeared once more, having been heard of for the last time in 1296, blessing and consecrating the rising star of William Wallace. According to eye-witnesses a hare was actually seen in the ruins of the Rhymer's tower in 1839, "Sure enough," said one of them, "there it was — two young hares in a nettle bush in the fireplace."

Scott went on to describe the site of the original Celtic monastery of Old Melrose which lay below them. It was at the door of this monastery that the young shepherd Cuthbert had knocked for admittance. And it was to that monastery that a charter was given by Petrus de Haga, promising the annual gift of half a stone of wax. That charter replaced an earlier undertaking to provide every year "ten salmon to wit, five fresh and five old [preserved] for ever". The reason for the alteration of the original terms of agreement have never been explained, but the charter is interesting because it provides the only evidence of the actual existence of Thomas the Rhymer.

The deed was made between 1260 and 1270, some time after the building and founding of the later Abbey of Melrose. Perhaps it had some connection with a special dispensation for members of the Haig family. Perhaps even the story of the monk who "formed an intimacy with one of the ladies of Bemersyde which was inconsistent with his vows as a celebate and his marriage to the Church" had some connection to it. According to the legend, the lady then mysteriously disappeared and the monk "was condemned to bathe every day throughout the year in penance of his fault". Ever since, the poor lady's ghost has haunted the pool below Bemersyde — on moonlit November nights she is wont to appear from beneath the surface of the river and gives a piercing scream. She then disappears and the waters come together above her head.

Listening to Scott's descriptions that he was unable to draw, all the time Turner's mind was absorbing the view of the bends of the river below. He could see its course from the Peeblesshire hills in the right-hand distance past the steep banks below, and on again flowing in a temporary direction towards the Teviotdale hills to the left. Scott's descriptions of romances with fairies and love affairs with monks kindled the imagination of Turner. A touch of the magic spell came upon him, and when Scott described the Rhymer's Glen, which lay over the shoulder of the right-hand Eildon and which is said to have led into Fairyland, Turner expressed a strong desire to see it. The following evening his desire was to be fulfilled in an unexpected way.

The morning of the next day, Sunday, the third day of the visit, was spent near Bowhill, where Turner was struck by the turns of the Yarrow Water and confessed that "he could have gloated over the beauties of it for a whole day". With his expert eye for a good composition, he drew Newark Castle from the opposite bank of the river and he used these drawings later on for the vignette in Volume VI of the *Poetical Works*.

Turner arrived back at Abbotsford in time to change before leaving with Scott, Cadell, and Scott's younger daughter Anne, to dine with the Lockharts at Chiefswood. John Gibson Lockhart was Scott's son-in-law, married to Charlotte, and their house at the foot of the Rhymer's Glen was adjacent to Abbotsford. There was time before dinner to make a drawing of the house from which later a watercolour was made now in the Vaughan Collection. As soon as dinner was over, Turner set off with Scott's two daughters, Mrs Lockhart and Anne, to explore up the Rhymer's Glen. He had drunk a fair amount of wine at dinner and, perhaps as a result, found it difficult to negotiate the rather slippery rocks of the burn. According to Cadell, he finally emerged from the glen rather tired and with wet feet. One wonders how much help the Scott girls had been — they must have seen the funny side of the painter's debacle! On their return to Abbotsford, Turner berated Cadell for leaving him for so long in the glen alone with the young women. Cadell explained that he had made an effort to find him but since no one had answered his call he had returned to the house. Turner staggered off to bed — but not before accidentally lurching into a bedroom that was not his own.

The plan for the last day of Turner's tour, Monday 8th August 1831, was to visit both Dryburgh Abbey and Melrose Abbey. Scott had accepted an invitation to dine that evening with James Haig at Bemersyde. Turner decided to turn down the invitation, anxious to make the most of his last day in the Borders country. He missed an enjoyable evening, since James Haig was a good companion who had travelled widely and spent some years in Rome. His claret was well known, and his daughter Barbara entertained the company with songs after dinner. Scott regarded that as a mixed blessing. He had already written in his Journal — "Miss Haig sings Italian music better than any person I ever heard out of the Opera House. But I am neither a judge nor admirer of the science. I do not know exactly what is aimed at, and therefore cannot tell what is attained." The dining room was in the old peel tower, the walls of which are between seven and eleven feet thick into which the windows are recessed. These windows date from the seventeenth century, when Antony Haig, whose mother came from Holland, redesigned the room giving it a Dutch atmosphere. There is, in one of these windows, a family coat of arms, rendered in stained glass, with the motto *"Come what will"*, a variation of Thomas the Rhymer's prophecy. The two old friends were glad to be together. Although Scott was no longer his convivial self, he enjoyed talking to James about happenings on their estates and about friends and neighbours. Each of them was a keen and knowledgeable agriculturalist who had improved his land. Each had planted woods and drained fields and improved yields. In their younger days, each had served in the forces. With many things in common, these two men of fine intellect, sense of humour, and deep humanity, enjoyed a close relationship, and it is sad to think that when Scott left Bemersyde that evening, frail and tired, it may well have been for the last time.

Meanwhile, early that morning, Turner and Cadell had been up at five-thirty and ready by seven-fifteen to get into Scott's gig, drawn by two fast ponies in tandem. After breakfast at Drygrange, they reached the swing bridge at Dryburgh by nine-fifteen and instructed the driver of the gig to meet them at St Boswells at midday. They then crossed the river to the Abbey, built beside another horseshoe bend of the Tweed in a setting of magnificent old trees. At first sight the visitor is shocked by the extent of the ruination of the Abbey, which was attacked three times by the English invaders. On the third occasion it was reduced to a ruin. The Abbey had been built for the Premonstratension canons in the year 1150 by Hugo de Morville and his wife, Beatrix de Bello. It is probable that Petrus de Haga, the first laird of Bemersyde, had a hand in the foundation, since he is believed to have come from Casp de la Hague in Normandy with Hugo de Morville. They had stopped for a while on the way to Scotland at a place in Dorset, where their names are recorded. The canons had arrived from the Abbey of Alnwick in Northumberland, where a monastery of Premonstratensians had existed for thirty years. The priorities of these canons who lived at Dryburgh during the early period of its existence were prayer, reading and contemplation. The spectacle of the White Fathers at their devotions must have been moving. The practice of woshipping seven times each day meant their getting up at least once during the night, and processing, candles alight, down the stairs from the adjacent dormitories into the Church of St Mary. Labouring on the land was considered a distraction, and as there was no drainage in the fields the production was low, so it was just as well that the fathers were strict vegetarians.

Gradually, as farming methods improved and more land was made available to them, and thanks to regular gifts from members of my family and others, the Abbey lands became prosperous. And it was these riches in stock and crop that enticed men to cross the border and carry out their attacks, described so vividly in James Bulloch's *Adam of Dryburgh*.

> "In 1544 Hertford's cavalry were at Dryburgh but the place suffered little. Some months later, on Friday 4 November 1544, Sir George Bowes, Sir Brian Layton, and some 700 men '. . . rode into Scotland, upon the water of Tweide to a town called Dryburgh with an abbey in the same, which was a pretty town and well buylded; and they burnte the same town and abbey, saving the churche, with a great substance of corne and gote very much spoylage and insicht geir and brought away an hundredth nolte, sixty nagges, a hundredth sheipe . . . and they tarried so long at the said burnynge and spoylage that it was Satterday at eight of the cloke at nycht or they come home'."

After the Reformation the estate was erected into a temporal lordship and given to the Erskine family. The Abbey lands later passed to Thomas Haliburton, husband of Margaret Craig of Bemersyde, from whom Sir Walter Scott was descended. But for an extravagant grand-uncle who became bankrupt and had to part with the property, they would have descended to Sir Walter by inheritance. "We have nothing left of Dryburgh," he wrote, "but the right of stretching our bones there." Sadly, the day when he himself would exercise that right was not far off.

Turner admired the beauty of St Mary's aisle, where Scott was soon to lie, and the colour of the pink sandstone ruins around it. He explored the cloister and the chapter and warming houses leading off it, and made notes in his sketchbook of many of the architectural details of pillars and gables and of the ancient yew and cedar trees surrounding them. Having made these studies, he crossed over to the other side of the river by boat and then climbed the high bank beyond, on the outskirts of St Boswells village. Here he found a fine panorama, with the river in the foreground doing the same kind of loop as further up, beneath Scott's View, round to the Abbey parklands and woods, from which he had just come. From this viewpoint he was able to sketch the Eildons in the distance to the left, and, on the right, the high ground where stood the statue of William Wallace, recently put there by Lord Buchan.

In the final print, which forms the frontispiece of Volume V of the *Poetical Works*, the landscape has been romanticised, but is reasonably accurate from a topogrpahical point of view. As a fisherman, Turner had understood every variant of the river-flow beneath him and introduced two fishermen remarkably similar to those who wade the river for salmon today. In the far distance one sees the Battery Pool and Dryburgh Haugh, once part of Bemersyde Estate before it was presented to the monks, where the river flows down to the bottom left-hand end of the picture, to Harecraig and Burnfoot. In the foreground, to the right, boys are paddling near the side of Brockies Hole where the river bends towards a plane of light where it flattens and then runs over the cauld and out of the picture towards the Ash Tree pool.

Interestingly, Turner decided to devote his attention to the wide panoramas around Dryburgh, as he was also to do at Melrose, rather than give a detailed rendering of architecture. He was captivated by this river landscape.

The gig was waiting for him on the green at St Boswells, and after a picnic lunch, which he may well have munched on the journey, he reached Melrose Abbey at two-fifteen. Here he made the most elaborate architectural studies of his tour, labouring for three hours on three drawings which are a *tour de force* of accurate observation and of distilled vision. They were carried out when he was at his peak as a portrayer of landscape. There were no stumbles and no hesitations in the exercise of direct observation and notation with the aid of simple pencil.

After all this work, Turner was still ready to carry on and decided to return to the viewpoint on the far side of the river, near

Dryburgh Abbey from an etching by Turner.

Gattonside, from which he had seen the Abbey two days earlier. This meant a long haul in the gig, round by the bridge, but he knew that the view was suitable for the purposes of his illustration and that the light was good. The decision was right, as proved by the magnificent watercolour, now in the Vaughan Collection in Edinburgh, which emerged from the sketch. The engraving for Volume VI of the *Poetical Works* was based on that watercolour. In it Turner has shown Sir Walter and his party picnicking above the river, although in fact only Turner and Cadell and the pony boy had their dinner there that evening. No doubt Turner remembered the scene of two days earlier, when they had passed by on their way ot Smailholm. On this second visit Turner had to climb much further down the bank in order to find his viewpoint. Such an effort would have been too much for Scott in his frail state. The pony boy is shown sitting in the gig, which has a strange appearance — more like a tumbril used in the French Revolution. Again, the study is amazingly accurate from the topographical point of view, and Turner has managed to put his finger on one of the few ready-made subjects which are to be found in the Borders.

While Scott was already in the middle of dinner at Bemersyde, Turner was still not finished and set off again at seven-thirty along the road towards Galashiels. Without crossing the roadbridge near the Pavilion, he turned down left-handed over the Gala Water in order to view Abbotsford from below the Galashiels-Selkirk road. From there he was able to execute a drawing which was to be used for a delightful vignette in Volume XII of the *Poetical Works*, showing

Cadell and himself crossing over the river in the gig on their way home to Abbotsford after a hard day. There was a moon rising behind Abbotsford and the hour was late. They were tired. Their day out had lasted twelve and a half hours.

Thus ended the final episode of a successful and fruitful visit.

Next morning at breakfast Turner talked to Scott and to Cadell about the work he had achieved and about future plans. In the words of Gerald Finlay, "Scott found Turner a different man from what he had expected. Turner was very co-operative and cheerful, and was thoroughly enraptured by the gentle, rolling countryside of the Vale of Tweed. It is likely that Scott was taken with Turner's immediate and constant enthusiasm for scenery, whether it was a ruin, or the turn of a river."

Having established a good rapport with his host and having thoroughly enjoyed his visit, Turner set off for Berwick at one o'clock. After a short stay there to make some drawings for the publication, he left to visit the Highlands.

A few days later Scott wrote to Cadell who was then in Edinburgh.

> "My compliments to Mr Turner. Miss Mary Craig (of Bemersyde) was quite disappointed at not finding him here yesterday. I trust Mr Turner's journey [north] will be as successful as it has been, more so it can not be."

Sadly, Scott was never able to see the fruits of the visit. He suffered a serious stroke, and it was felt that a change of air and a rest from his work in a warmer climate might do something for him. So that autumn he set off on a tour of the Mediterranean in an attempt to mend his health. That was not to be. On July 11th 1832, he returned to Abbotsford. In the words of John Buchan, "That was all but the last gleam of light". He died in the early afternoon of September 21st. His funeral cortege passed by his favourite view on Bemersyde Hill and at that point, now known as Scott's View, the horses, which in happier times had been driven there with the sociable, stopped of their own accord. In the presence of a vast crowd of mourners he was buried by right of his Haliburton blood in the ruined Abbey of Dryburgh. A century later another great Borderer was brought from Bemersyde to be near him. That was my father, Douglas Haig. As the shadows move slowly across the faces of the sundial the Rhymer's prophetic words still hold true. Time passes by, generations come and go but the work of the Poet and the Painter and the Rhymer will endure forever.

Barefoot Jock

Lt. Col. Campbell Adamson

CARESTON

Caraldstone was part of a line of castles protecting the River South Esk, joined with Finhaven, Kinnaird, Albar, Forfar, Kinnardy and many others against the marauding savages of Aberdeenshire. North of them was another line — Cortachy, Invernak, Inverquharty and Edzell — and to the south, in case of an attack from the sea, Ethie, Usan and again many others along the coast.

Of all these castles Caraldstone was the oldest. Here, 700 years ago, the judge, or Judrex, of Angus or maybe even of all Scotland, a loon called Dempster, had built himself a small castle. It was only one room wide with walls four to five feet thick. He had called it Caraldstone after a Danish chieftain, or perhaps after Carril, an Ossian hero, both killed in the neighbourhood, with a stone there to commemorate the Danish defeat. His descendants had built a Tower House based on his little castle, only one room thick and facing north, from the top of which could be seen any folk coming from that direction.

Caraldstone was a defensive castle with three stone spiral staircases all clockwise to those attacking, making defence easier. Only one, the central one, reached to the ground, the other two stopped at the first storey and entry to them was only possible by ladders or from rooms leading to the central staircase. It was within this ancient fortification that our story begins.

It was 1453, although the young boy did not know the date. The summer sunshine had woken him early. He slept at the very top of the castle, on the fifth floor in a bed-box — a large cupboard which held two wooden bunks, one above the other. Jock's bed was the lower one because he was only sixteen, the other occupant being a year older. It was his duty, when the weather was cold, to snib the

Jock's bed-box

door of the cupboard when they were both bedded. It was not really a bad bedroom. It was dry, with two small eye windows and even a fireplace, although it was an effort to bring wood up to such a height — no coal was allowed of course. The room was protected from draughts by a door which led to the attic where the rafters could be seen; these were made of oak, only twelve inches apart with never a nail in them — only wooden pegs.

Soon, he hoped, he would join the other servants — those who slept on the ground floor. For that was how the defence of the castle was set up. The older and better servants slept on the ground floor; on the first floor was the Great Hall where the Lord and Lady entertained around the fireplace from a fire lit on the ground floor, its heat being increased by fireplaces in the Hall. The next two storeys above were where the gentry slept and above them slept the junior servants, so that the Lord and Lady were protected, or "sandwiched", by their servants.

The boy's name was Jock and he knew his nickname was "Barefoot Jock". In those days none save the gentry wore shoes except in winter, but Jock never wore shoes at any time — nor would he wear a bonnet even in the coldest winter months.

Jock was the Orra-boy, ordered to come and to go as the Steward of the Castle demanded. He received no wage, but he had food and a roof over his head. He knew that he was better off than most boys of his age as he was the elder son of the Quarry Master at the red sandstone quarry about a mile away, from which the castle and most of the buildings in the district had been built.

The sun was now higher in the sky and the day warmer, so Jock got out of his bed and made his way downstairs. His first duty every day was to draw water from the castle well and pour it into the barrels outside the kitchen. The well was not in the castle itself but placed within the outer defensive wall. Even in the summer the well never dried up although the water did become very low and not all that clean. When he had done this, Jock went into the castle for his breakfast. This was held in Dempster's "Little Castle" — a dark and gloomy place as the walls were so thick the sun never shone into it. But in winter it was the warmest place in the castle as the great fire was lit here. The food was always the same, pairritch made of oats with rye-bread, sour and black looking. The men drank weak ale whilst the queys drank water. "Pease broth with maybe a piece of braxy mutton and endless salmon," said Jock to himself as he thought about the monotony of the food and how he loathed it.

Sometime later in the morning, the steward called to him to take a message to Earl "Beardie Crawford", the Laird of Finhaven, also known as "The Tiger Earl", who lived on the other side of the South Esk about five miles away. The message was verbal as the Earl was not a great one for reading or writing. "Fine," thought Jock, "I can idle the day awa' and keep frae any work hereby." He took "a piece" from the kitchen table and wandered down the loan on the south side of the castle, repeating the message time and time again to himself in case he should forget it.

"What a castle Caraldstone is!" he said as he made his way down to the river past the well-kept and impressive fortifications. He passed a Spanish chestnut tree that had just been planted, grown from a chestnut from the Laird of Finhaven's "Great Tree". A Roman soldier had planted that tree, so folk said — not that Jock knew anything about the Romans but "they were once fierce men wha' raged round Scotland mony years afore".

He made his way down to the Norrin Burn, about a mile south of the castle, not a great burn but pleasant enough — "sae clean that the Queen of Scotland used to wash her linen in it, and mony mair besides her". How the touchats flew round about him and the whaups as well. There were sea-trout in the burn and maybe he would see a salmon in the river. He moved down to the north bank of the Norrin and just a short distance below where it flowed into the South Esk he crossed the river by the ford which the Romans had used on their way to the King's ford over the North Esk at Stracathro. From there he saw the remains of the castle guarding the ford.

An easy way for him now — only four miles up the river before he would come to Finhaven and he could reach the castle before having to cross the Lemno burn — a silly piece of water, muddy and difficult to cross. As at Caraldstone, the defensive wall round Finhaven was close to the castle itself. The policies were easy to enter, and here was the great Spanish chestnut tree itself, the one planted by the Roman soldier. As always, Jock looked at it in amazement; it was known as the Laird's Tree, and what a size it was! There was a broken branch hanging down and as he paused for a well-earned rest, Jock thought to himself, "It will make me a guid walking stick". After all he had been up for six or seven hours, walked for five miles and had even forgotten to eat his piece. He was feeling tired, so he took out the knife that he always carried (his father had given it to him on his fourteenth birthday) and fashioned the branch into a walking stick.

As Jock worked on the branch he suddenly became conscious of two men approaching him, one bearded and well clad and the other obviously a superior servant. "God's wounds," said the well-clad man, "who in the name of the Devil are you?"

Jock, recognising a gentry, bobbit his head and said, "I have a message for the Earl of Crawford from Dempster of Caraldstone."

"I am the Earl of Crawford and what in God's name is that stick you have? Taken it from my ain tree, have you?" Then turning to his servant he said, "The lad must be hangit — string him up from the tree."

"My Lord," said the servant, "this is unjust and unreasonable, at least let him deliver his message."

"St Michael and all the Angels!" said the Earl. "String him up. I will not deal with such trash."

And so the fourth Earl of Crawford, the Tiger Earl, had young Barefoot Jock hanged from the great Spanish chestnut tree at Finhaven. His body was buried in a shallow grave on the north side of the great tree, the area where all nondescript persons were buried.

Careston Castle

After his unhappy death, Jock did not, however, make his final exit from the life of the castle. He lived on in the spirit world and his ghost was witness to many changes in the fortunes of Caraldstone, whose name over the years changed to Careston.

Its southern approach had been planted out with a great avenue of lime trees. On the west side a walled garden was made and in front a deerpark. New lairds moved in — the Lindsays, who were big landowners and implemented more improvements in the building to match their prestige. In 1700 the great hall was divided into a dining room and a with-drawing room, with a small chapel constructed between them.

With the arrival of the Stewarts of Grantully at Careston, the Royal Coat of Arms of Scotland was put in the drawing room and their own coat of arms on the front of the castle. The daughter of the next owners, the Skenes, married the Earl of Fife, who went bankrupt and in 1872 the estate passed into the hands of the Adamsons. By this time repairs were long overdue; the new owners married with the Campbells of Stracaltro and once again Jock made his presence felt to a generation enjoying a time of prosperity, bringing with it such modernisations as electricity. This union between the two Scottish families explains the name of the present occupants of the house — the Campbell Adamsons.

To this day Jock's bed-box at the top of the castle is still reserved for its now ancient dweller. Some folk have tried to move in. One lad from England took a bet that he could spend the night in Jock's bed and took a bottle of whisky with him for courage. Next morning there was no sign of the lad, just an empty bottle of whisky!

It is said that Jock will remain at Careston, his "former habitation", until the message he was carrying on that fateful day is delivered to the descendants of the fourth Earl of Crawford. But the message will never be delivered: the Earl's family has ceased to exist. But Jock probably rests in greater peace than the tyrant "auld Beardie" who had him hanged. It is said the Earl haunts Glamis Castle as the "Monster of Glamis" where he is condemned to play cards in a small room to the time of Judgement.

"Earl Beardie willna dee
Nor puir Jock Barefoot be set free
As long as grows a Chestnut tree."

The Life and Times of Dame Muriel of Cawdor

The Earl of Cawdor

CAWDOR

A Victorian chronicler, discussing the Cawdor family history at the opening of the sixteenth century, wrote with inspired understatement:

> "The next step . . . is involved in some curious difficulties."

William, Thane of Cawdor, owned large estates. By 1493 he was an old man and decided to arrange his succession. His eldest son William being weak, lame and "inclined to the Church", was set aside with a pension in favour of the second son, John. The ageing Thane had married off John to Isabella, daughter of Hugh, Baron Rose of Kilravock, an arranged marriage intended to end a long-standing feud between two neighbouring and powerful houses. Kilravock Castle is a couple of miles as the east wind blows from Cawdor Castle, rather too close for proud, quarrelsome families to live in anything other than a state of tension.

At this period of Scottish history, the surviving families standing were educated pirates; with knowledge both of Latin and the law, they had learned the value of legal ties, yet were not slow when all else failed to resort to rope and dirk, poison and arson. As one later Rose laird explained it to the King, his bad neighbours were his good neighbours because they made him go thrice a day to God on his knees. That the Roses and Cawdors were fierce is not in doubt; their actions went beyond quibbles and "high debates"; in 1482, Cawdor was an accomplice in storming and taking Kilravock Castle, while young Rose was held in the dungeon at Cawdor; in the last decade of the fifteenth century, both family chiefs and their heirs were remitted from sentence to the block for multiple murders.

Against this background, when John Cawdor died prematurely in the summer of 1497 leaving his young wife "big of twins", serious problems loomed for the old Thane and his brothers, and the worst was confirmed when twin girls, Muriel and Janet, were born on 13 February 1498. Within two days the Thane had drawn up a document seeking to prove bastardy (based on an alleged verbal deathbed statement by his son) and sealed "at about 10 o'clock" in his castle chapel, dedicated suitably enough to the Blessed Virgin. In this ugly endeavour he was supported by his devout uncle, the Precentor of Ross, who was, comically, illegitimate himself. Janet died within a year of birth, leaving Muriel as sole heiress unless her legal claims could be overturned.

Archibald Campbell, 2nd Earl of Argyll, soon got wind of the child heiress. Moving with a speed which would leave modern lawyers breathless, he had in a matter of months obtained the gift of marriage and ward of Muriel, had become one of her legal governors, and lastly her chief attorney by Royal consent; at the same time he had confirmed his appointments with all the local sheriffs in the north-east, including the sheriff of Nairn — William Cawdor. As Argyll not only had the King's ear but held great sway in the country, he was easily able to out-manoeuvre the Cawdors legally. Moreover, he had leverage over Baron Rose who was conveniently under prosecution for cattle rustling, and obtained his ostensible agreement without difficulty. In return he gave Rose a Bond of Friendship, a much favoured Scots document that frequently turned out to be perfectly worthless: long on words, short on intent, massive in fees. Argyll was as a tiger amidst mewling wildcats. He was not only crafty, but brave and intelligent; and he held three aces: he was Master of the King's Household, Chancellor, and Lord Chamberlain. Muriel, during all this frantic activity, had been taken to Kilravock Castle and placed under the watchful eye of her grandparents.

Lord Argyll was adept at the Campbell skill of "fishing in troubled waters". It must have occurred to him that Muriel's future was still in doubt. Rose had private designs of marrying her to one of his grandsons; the Cawdors were still contesting her legitimacy in the courts, and even if that attempt failed, assassination might succeed. The then Argyll motto was, "I bide my time". But he did not wait long. Judging that the girl would be strong enough to survive the trek over to the west and that the weather might be fair, at harvest time in 1499, without warning, he sent sixty men under Campbell of Inverliver to collect Muriel from Kilravock and bring her back to Inveraray Castle for safekeeping.

According to family tradition, Muriel had to be removed by force and that for future recognition of the child her grandmother branded her hip with the key of her coffer and her nurse bit off the top joint of her left-hand little finger. The Campbell party, carrying their valuable but wounded cargo, set off homewards. A few miles from Kilravock, while fording the River Nairn at Daltulich, they were overtaken by a large Cawdor posse. The Campbells had removed Muriel's outer clothes, dresed up a sheaf of oats as a feint, sent the child on with half a dozen men as an escort, and then the rest faced the angry uncles and their followers to protect the dummy in a bloody battle. During the skirmish, seven or eight of Inverliver's sons were killed, and it is said that in desperation Campbell of Inverliver cried out in Gaelic, "It's a far cry to Lochawe!" — according to one historian the origin of the expression. Anyway, as usual, Campbell's deception worked, their surviving party beat a

Cawdor Castle

retreat and Inverliver limped back to Inveraray and was handsomely rewarded for the successful mission.

Lord Argyll was censured by the elders of his clan for pointless loss of life should the injured and exhausted heiress of seventeen months die, to which his answer is supposed to have been that Muriel of Cawdor would never die so long as there was a red-haired lassie on the shores of Loch Fyne.

By March 1502, Argyll had tied up his legal knots tightly. All the Cawdors' cases, including unfair trial, had been thrown out, and Muriel was confirmed before the Provost of Edinburgh's court as rightful heir. More than that, she was safely installed in Argyll's castle, then a comparatively new house.

Under the powerful wing of Argyll, Muriel grew up at Inveraray. Legal age was then twelve; the Earl, nothing if not a slouch, provided Muriel with her own wax seal, and with her own husband in the form of his third son, Sir John Campbell, by Elizabeth, daughter of the Earl of Lennox. On 17 February 1511, under her own seal, she invested her husband with her lands and property. This document was witnessed at the "lordly eagle's nest commanding a matchless stretch of country", Castle Campbell.

Muriel reinforced her security against her aggressive relations in the east by resigning her personal Thanedom in favour of herself and her protective spouse at the palace of Holyroodhouse on 3 March 1511, again using her pretty new seal. It would be neat to suppose that she lived happily ever after but she was fated never to be far from violence, legend, death and disruption.

Muriel's grandfather, Thane William of Cawdor, had died about 1503. That same year his bastard uncle, the Precentor, perhaps recognising the importance of blankets, had obtained letters under the Great Seal for his own legitimation, and was at pains to prepare plans and buy land in order to bolster the cause and the forlorn claims to the thanedom of his nephew, Hugh Cawdor, who had been assigned by his brother Sir William, the sheriffdom of Nairn, the Constabulary of the King's castle and other county pickings and perquisites. As late as 1500, William Cawdor records a legal protest in writing and as a token of revocation, "breaks this dish with fire, with my own foot, as custom is . . .", or as pagan habit was, and hardly up to the expectation of a vicar and certainly nowhere near as efficient as Campbell litigation.

Over on the west coast of Scotland, Muriel may have enjoyed a year or more of tranquillity. Archibald, Earl of Argyll, who had acted as her first mentor, protector, provider and "eagle", was killed at Flodden Field in September 1513. The next elder brother, Colin, became Earl, and Muriel's husband increased his ambitions as he moved up a notch. From this period, Dame Muriel and Sir John apparently lived at Muckairn in Lorn, which was technically an offshoot of the property of the Bishops of Iona, if not in practice.

Sir John acquired the land of Muckairn finally by writ in 1532. Long before that, he seems to have resided there as Baillie with his child-bride, and the method of gaining possession is preserved, in a diverting if unconvincing fable, which runs like this:

> legend says that the men of both parties assembled on a field, near Kilmaronag, and that the two commanders (MacDougall of Lorne and the "Lord" of Cawdor) walked a bit to the south of the field of the battle to make an armistice, and gave orders to the men when they left, not to stir until they saw them lift their swords — when a serpent came out of a bush and they lifted their swords to kill it. The men, seeing their swords up, took it for a signal of attack, and fought until there were but two left, each by the name of John. On the way they cast out; the one killed the other. When MacDougall gave up Muckairn to "Lord" Cawdor, as the chiefs agreed before the serpent appeared, one of the conditions was that Cawdor be kind to MacDougall's vassals whom he left on it. . . .

Across the waters of Loch Etive from Muckairn lies the Isle of Mull. The Maclean chieftain there was Lachlan Cattenach of Duart who was married to Lady Elizabeth, Sir John Campbell's sister. Maclean, having decided to rid himself of his wife in the least agreeable way, had Elizabeth chained naked to "the Lady's Rock" in the Firth of Lorn between Duart Castle and the island of Lismore. She might die of exposure, failing which high tide would drown her slowly. In the event, she was rescued by some passing fishermen who thought they saw a large white sea-bird, and took her back by boat to her brother's house. Muriel's husband avenged this cruelty by dirking Maclean to death in bed in Edinburgh "under cloud and silence of night", on 10 November 1524. King James V gave remission to Sir John for this murder in December the following year and for burning the Maclean lands of Colonsay.

This episode began a deadly and lasting feud between the

Campbells and the Macleans. Governments were not above using this type of hereditary hatred to their advantage; for example, it was hardly a coincidence that a hundred and fifty years later, in 1674, Sir Hugh Campbell of Cawdor was ordered by the Privy Council to act as one of the Commissioners to pursue to the death "with Fire and Sword" the Macleans of Duart. Sir Hugh appears to have taken not the slightest notice of these instructions. To complete the digression, it is noteworthy that the present noble Laird of Duart rose to be Chief Scout.

To return; this same incident seems to have been instrumental in determining Sir John to remove his wife Muriel and their family from the west and to make Cawdor their home. "Make" was the word, because when Sir John and Muriel arrived at her castle in the expectation of more peace and fewer Macleans, the Cawdor uncles were by no means friendly.

In fact the late Thane William's brothers were all hostile. Hugh was sheriff of Nairn, William was still Vicar, and Andrew was plainly dangerous, judging by a note:

> During Muriel's residence in Argyll, her uncle, a very ferocious man, was guilty of various acts of robbery and murder; the people dreaded him so much that they sent for the swiftest persons they could find from other quarters to apprehend him, but he was so swift of foot that he could run two miles to their one. At last he was outlawed, and a reward offered to any person that would take him dead or alive. In the course of his rounds, he came down the shoulder of the hill of Orkney (Urchany) by the castle of Rait, and concealed himself behind a large stone near the water dam there, when a man near the place observed him looking over the stone; and the man having a loaded gun, shot him in the forehead, the only part of that was visible of him above the stone. . . .

This has the ring of truth. Another note is more fanciful:

> After this marriage (to Muriel), Sir J. Campbell continued his own sirname and did not assume that of Cawdor as is frequently done by those who marry Heiresses whereby he seemed rather to found a new family than continue an old one which was occasioned by his being supported by the Campbells against the constant insult of the Cawdors for several ages and

> that so exasperated (were) the Heirs Male and relations of the name of Cawdor that they had constant feuds and skirmishes with the Campbells of Cawdor for a considerable time and carried off all the ancient writings belonging to the Family which are since either lost or destroyed and this in great measure has occasioned the original Transactions of the family of Cawdor to be in so much obscurity.

Yet another family scribbler records that the end of the feud was resolved by one brave man:

> This Donald MacAlester Roy, as he was called was a man of uncommon spirit and activity, and was a great service and use to the Family he sprung from.

(He may have been an illegitimate son of Sir John's, or he may have been, like the unicorn, a mythical beast. The family historian wishes him upon Sir John's third son, in which case this hero would at the time have been in nappies.)

> The Cawdors haivng laid siege to the Castle of Cawdor, he (Roy) sallied out against them, slew the chief of the Cawdors and his brother, with his own hand, and, by that action, raised the siege.

So if that is true, he must have killed Muriel's uncle Andrew and either the Revd. William, or Hugh the sheriff, who is recorded as graveyard dead in 1529. None of this is impossible to believe in when taking into consideration the high-handed standards of Scottish behaviour of the time.

What is certain is that Muriel and Sir John settled in at Cawdor. He had winkled the sheriffdom out of Uncle Hugh, with his spouse's (Muriel's) consent, in exchange for some life-rented land in High's favour, free, except for "one red rose if it be desired". This formal contract was signed at Stirling in 1528. After that, they set about putting their house and estate in order, and in Campbells' fashion increasing the size and value of their property as the influence and grip of the old Cawdor line dwindled and collapsed in the district.

The provision, "with his spouse's consent", hints that Sir John and Muriel had become a close, formidable couple. His brother Colin, the 3rd Earl of Argyll, had died in 1529, to be succeeded by his son Archibald; and by now Muriel, in contrast to her fragile and perilous start in life, was connected to almost every great family in Scotland.

During all this time, Muriel had borne and reared a family of five sons and six daughters, and the latter must have been quite handsome: the eldest married first Lord Ogilive and at his death, Lord Crawford; the others eventually became Lady Lovat, Lady Ross, Lady Fife, Lady Rattray and Lady Tolly — altogether a quiver of arrows.

Once established at Cawdor, Sir John, who seems to have possessed the stamina and determination of a Roman centurion, had quickly organised legal pacts of friendship with his old enemies and new neighbours both in the west and at Cawdor, even with the young Baron Rose of Kilravock. He now set upon one last mysterious land conquest, and he did so using one of the clan's unwritten rules: if you cannot take it, destroy it and buy it.

He had his eye on the Lindsays' property in Strathnairn, and so he burnt their Castle of Daviot to the ground, slew two of the servants and took their cattle.

Sir John, now sheriff of Nairn, was tried in October 1534 for these crimes under the auspices of the Lord Justice General, his nephew, the new Earl of Argyll. Declining to try his own uncle at Inverness, Argyll fielded another relation, Sir John Campbell of Lundy, as his deputy. This family party resulted in acquittal.

By November of the next year, Sir John had acquired the whole barony of Strathnairn from David, Earl of Crawford, for the sum of one thousand pounds "gold and silver usual money of Scotland". To modern thought this was skulduggery. Yet Muriel's family were able to smooth out the lumps of trickery: in 1549, Katherine of Cawdor married the next Earl of Crawford, lived happily at Edzell Castle in Angus, where her coat of arms is still to be seen in the garden.

With the death of Muriel's uncle Hugh, the old direct male line of the Cawdors ceased. There was brief family calm and routine until the year 1537. Muriel's brother-in-law, her husband's elder brother, Archibald Campbell of Skipnish, had married Janet, Lady Glamis. Lord Glamis had died young in 1527 at the age of thirty-seven, after which Janet was "much courted by the nobility", and a few years later chose Archibald. In the eyes of some she had two abiding sins, first that she was a Douglas and, secondly, she was a singularly beautiful woman; according to one opinion "the most celebrated beauty in the nation"; to make matters worse, she was also brave, clever, virtuous, generous, unblemished and chaste.

Her brother, the Earl of Angus, had been deposed as Chancellor of Scotland, forfeited and exiled in 1528; he had married Margaret, James IV's Queen Dowager, and thus was King James V's stepfather and an object of abject hatred in Royal circles. As a signal for this implacable vengeance towards the Douglases in general and Lady Janet in particular, a footling accusation was made of her "Using Charms against her husband" in 1532. This case, based on veiled charges of witchcraft, failed as had several previously abortive attempts to indict her for treason, mainly because no jurors could be found to perjure themselves.

The new proceedings against Lady Janet also involved her husband Archibald and her son, John Lord Glamis, who was still a boy. The accusations were conspiracy to murder the King by poison, and for treason in assisting and "communing" with her brothers. These charges were drubbed up by William Lyon, a cousin of the late Lord Glamis. Lyon's motive was not political. It was founded upon unrequited lust for Lady Janet. Lyon at Court had stirred up the King's unmanly fear of anyone of the Douglas tribe.

When brought to the Bar on 17 July 1537, Lady Janet answered her accusers with such eloquence and manifest honesty that the judges, although clearly convinced of her innocence, hid behind their robes and advised the King that "they were tied up to the form and letter of the law". Their cowardice allowed them only so far as to point out that clemency belonged to the King, who ignobly replied that "he knew nothing that could hinder them from doing their duty like men of judgement and honour", both of which attributes were wide of the mark. The judges were given full power to proceed with Lady Janet's execution without one shred of evidence:

> ". . . she shall be had to Castle hill in Edinburgh, and there BURNT in a fire to the death, as a Traitor. AND that I give for Doom."

So, lovely and courageous to the end, Lady Janet was burnt at the stake.

The mob had tried unsuccessfully to rescue her, but the ignorant supposed that she had been burnt for witchcraft, an art they held in as great terror as did his Majesty.

Her husband, her son and her elderly chaplain (a kinsman) were all still incarcerated in Edinburgh Castle. The day after his wife's nauseating trial and death, Archibald tried to escape, scaled the wall with too short a rope and falling onto the rocks, was "dashed to pieces" and killed. That same day, the pillars of justice tried young Lord Glamis for treason, and found him guilty and condemned him to be hanged and drawn. Glamis then was about eleven years old.

The more well informed were not content at the prospect of a nobleman's execution in his minority condemned on threadbare testimony. They also noted the absence from the proceedings of the Justiciar, Lady Janet's nephew, the Earl of Argyll, an absence not entirely explicable on the grounds of family bias, but something that insinuated that pure justice was not on display, rather the King's black venom. It was known that the King had vowed to "accomplish the ruin" of the Douglases and the house of Glamis. The King, aware of a rising tide of opinion and fury against these despicable injustices, released the old priest and communted Lord Glamis's death sentence to imprisonment.

On the pretext that John Lord Glamis could, as well he might if free, avenge the death of his mother upon the King, he was kept in prison until after the King's death. As for William Lyon, it is said that he died "in Flanders in misery". Neither he nor the King can have had consolation, at death, unless they were able to forget Lady Janet's final heroic words:

> . . . for my husband, son, and cousin are neither of that name or family (Douglas). I shall end my life with more comfort if you absolve them. For the more of us that suffer by your unjust sentence the greater will be your guilt, and more terrible your condemnation, when you shall be tried at the great day by the Almighty God, who is the impartial judge of all flesh.

The King, already ill, died in 1542 on hearing the news of the defeat of his army at Solway Moss.

To Muriel and Sir John, neither of them of sentimental cast, the brutal loss of their brother and sister-in-law must have been shattering, but life continued at Cawdor. In 1545, their son and heir married Isabel Grant of Castle Grant, and the following spring, on 1 May 1546, Sir John died.

Muriel was now in her forty-ninth year. Her son, the new Thane, did not live long, dying in 1551, leaving a son and daughter. Muriel was, for the era, beyond remarriage, and lived a private life at

Cawdor, watching the world go by and keeping a firm hold on her estates.

It was not long before her sleep may have been disturbed again. Her niece, Margaret Campbell of Cawdor, had married John Forbes of Towie. While Forbes was away, Adam Gordon of Auchindoune Castle taking up the vendetta between the Gordons and the clan Forbes, swooped down on Corgarff Castle in upper Strathdon in November 1571. Margaret resisted. Gordon set fire to the place. She, her three young children and her retainers were burnt, "in all twenty-seven people, to Ashes". Once again, the beauty of this woman was alleged to have been the central motive for mindless murder; Adam Forbes, enraged and shamed by his impotence in neither gaining access to her strong castle nor to her soft body, resorted to boastful barbarity.

The outrage was recorded in the ballad "Edom O' Gordon". There are several renderings of this traditional poem, set in different places and celebrating other people; the following edition is the Strathdon version, taken down verbatim as late as 1965, given by the then head gamekeeper, who had known it since childhood, and as he firmly believed, told "the truth of the matter":

It fell aboot the Martinmas time when the wind
blew shrill and cauld,
Says Edom o' Gordon to his men, "We maun draw
tae some hall."
"What hall, what hall, my merry men, what hall,
what hall," quo' he.
"I think we'll gong tae the Campbells' hoose
and see the fair lady."
She thocht it was her ain true lord that she
saw ridin' hame,
But it was that traitor Edom o' Gordon wha
rect' nae sin nor shame.
"Gie owre yer hoose, Lady Campbell," he cries.
"Gie owre the hoose tae me,
"Or I will burn you this nicht and a' yer
bairnies three."
"I winna gie owre my hoose," she cries, "tae
laird nor yet tae loon."

"Or tae any bank robber that comes frae
Achintoon."
The lady frae the battlements she let twa
bullets flee,
But it missed its mark wi' Gordon, for it
only grazed his knee.
"Come here, come here, no Captain Carr, tak
oot her Queerin' stanes,
"Come here, come here, no Captain Carr, and
fire at her let in."

Then up and spak her eldest son, on the castle
head stood he,
"I've shot wi' yer guns, mither, till I'm a'
brunt, fit and han',
"I've shot wi' yer guns, mither, till I can
nae longer stan'."
Up and spak her youngest son, sat on the
nurse's knee,
"Open the door and let me oot, for the reek
it's chokin' me."
"I wad gie a' ma gold, my child, my money
and my fee
"For a'e blast o' western win' tae blow
the reek frae thee."
Then spak she tae her dochter dear, the
bonniest o' them a',
"I'll rowe ye in a pair o' sheets and throw
ye owre the wa'."
They rowed her in a pair o' sheets and threw
her owre the wa',
But on the point o' Gordon's sword she got a
deadly fa'.
Syne Gordon turned her owre and owre and o'
her face was white.
"I micht a spared that bonnie face tae be
some man's delight."
And then he turned to his men, "Aye lads we
best awa',

"For the Campbells' hoose is in a blaze, nae
langer need we sta'."
Then up an' spak her ain true Lord, for on the
sea sailed he,
"Oh, bonnie Corgarff is a' on fire, could God
preserve my lady gay."
He lapped into the big, big fire, baith boots
and spurs an' a'.
And he stole a kiss o' his own true love and
her body fell in twa.
"Oh, I hae corn and I hae beer and barley in
a bing,
"But I would gie it a' this night tae hear
my lady sing."

At the age of seventy-five and heiress to far greater estates and possessions than those which had originally caused such clamour, Muriel felt the time was ripe to make over everything to her grandson, or as she charmingly puts it in Scots, to "John Campbell my oy". This she carried out with her usual efficiency in June 1573, signing herself Muriel Cawdor of that Ilk, demonstrating that she regarded Cawdor now very much as her home. It was witnessed by one of her Rose relations who were once more amicable. Whereas her exact day of birth is known, her precise year of death is not; it was probably about 1575. The old lady was no longer of avid interest to lawyers, lovers, kidnappers and gossips.

By the age of seventy-nine, she would have survived long enough to learn about the incredible plot to kill her daughter Marjory, Lady Ross, who had married George Ross, the Laird of Balnagowan. This murderous enterprise was engineered by Marjory's sister-in-law, Lady Katherine Ross and her (Katherine's) stepson, Hector Munro of Foulis. The objective was to "remove" Marjory, and then arrange the remarriage of George Ross to the wife of the heir to Foulis, Robert Og Munro, which plan required his "removal" also. The conspirators employed two highly respected witches, Marion "Burn-the-Ladle" MacAllister, and William "The Ox" MacGillivray, both senior members of the witches' coven at Tain. After a certain amount of capering about, shooting elf-arrows at clay images and other mumbo-jumbo, it was found, disappointingly, that none of this nonsense had the least effect on Lady Marjory who came from tough stock.

After all this witchcraft, incantation and sorcery had floundered so abysmally, the instigators became impatient, so The Ox lumbered off to Elgin for "a box of witchcraft", which was in fact rat poison. this was liberally used, but badly bungled. Many were only slightly poisoned; a nurse sent off in the dark with a more potent brew for dinner dropped the jar, breaking it, but tasted the new mixture "and immediately thereafter departed" (life), which at least raised the hopes of the plotters, and raised other questions which were hard, later, to answer. Finally, they managed to poison Marjory to the extent that she "contracted deadly sickness", and was alive but incurable as late as 1590 when the case came to court; a trial of textbook Mafia standards in which Hector Munro himself was the prosecutor and the "packed" jury was composed of Ross and Munro dependants. The Ox had been burnt to death in 1577, and Burn-the-Ladle either drowned or imprisoned; the ladies of high birth and low principles were acquitted in a trial superior to even Campbell manipulation.

At all events, Lady Muriel died quietly before she could mark another injustice to her kin. She was laid to rest in the family vault in Barevan Kirk, the church once the charge of her uncle and arch-enemy, he of the dish, the Revd. William.

In the seventeenth century, Sir Hugh Campbell of Cawdor saw fit to install a chimney-piece in his new dining room in the castle, carved from a single slab of sandstone, nine feet long, three feet high and more than a foot thick in the rough, and weighing several tons. This commemorates the marriage of Sir John Campbell and Lady Muriel Cawdor, and bears their joint coat of arms, their initials IC and MC, the date of their marriage, 1510, and in monogram SD for Sir and Dame. Beneath, in dog Latin runs the legend,

"In the morning remember your creator".
A pun of sorts.

Some Urquharts of Cromarty and Craigston

Bruce Urquhart

CRAIGSTON CASTLE

John Urquhart of Craigfintry, the youngest son of the senior branch of the Urquharts of Cromarty, being guardian of his great-great-nephew Sir Thomas, was known as the Tutor of Cromarty. He owned much land in Deveronside before choosing a site for his castle. The tower he built is sixty-seven feet high up to the crowning balustrade. A richly sculptured balcony features the boy David slinging at Goliath; a piper and other grotesque figures project over the entrance which is recessed into a great arch in the centre of which is a hole ideally suited for dropping boiling oil on unwelcome visitors to Craigston.

The Tutor married three times, one branch of his family continuing the Craigston Urquharts, while that of Cromarty ended its male line in 1741. The following melancholy ballad records the death of young orphaned John Urquhart of Cromarty and Craigston, whom his guardian stepfather married to his daughter Elizabeth.

Father, she said, you have done me wrong
For ye have married me on a child young man
For ye have married me on a child young man,
And my bonny love is long a growing.

Daughter, said he, I have done you no wrong
For I have married you on a heritor of land
He's likewise possess'd of many bill and banc
And he'll be daily growing.
Growing, deary, growing, growing
Growing, said the bonny maid,
Slowly's my bonny love growing.

Daughter, said he, if ye do weel
Ye will put your husband away to the scheel,
That he of learning may gather great skill,
And he'll be daily growing,
Growing, &c.

Now young Craigston to the College is gane
And left his lady making great mane
That he's so long a growing
Growing &c.

She dress'd herself in robes of green
They were right comely to be seen
She was the picture of Venus the Queen
And she's to the College to see him
Growing &c.

Then all the colleginers was playing at the ba'
But young Craigstone was the flower of them a'
He said — play on, my school fellows a'
For I see my sister coming.

Now down into the College park
They walked about till it was dark,
Then he lifted up her fine holland sark —
And she had no reason to complain of his growing
Growing &c.

In his twelfth year he was a married man,
In his thirteenth year there he got a son,
And in his fourteenth year his grave grew green,
And that was the end of his growing —
Growing, deary, &c.

As the current, unsolicited occupant of the castle, I am sitting in its library, comforted by shelves of leather-bound books and the faint smell of Neat's foot oil. I am out of range of telephone or television; I am at the top. I am thinking of William Urquhart of Craigston, whose handsome bookplates grace the volumes of Swift and Sterne, Adam Smith's *Wealth of Nations*, Evelyn's *Silva*, King James's Works and his counterblast to tobacco, and the works of philosophers and divines of Aberdeen University. As the sunset warms the room, I see the kestrel as usual, poised, about to dip into the arch below to his roost on the window ledge of the upstairs lavatory. Sleeping with its head under one wing, its headless image is apt to upset evening visitors to the loo. Which reminds me of my boyhood years of suffering from the strange sights and unaccountable sounds in the castle, shared by my mother and sisters and an occasional guest.

It was in 1917 that it started, when two tired but excited schoolboys alighted one winter evening at Plaidy Station near the end of the Great Northern Railway line to Banff. I was the nine-year-old heir to Craigston, the other was a school friend from Colet Court. Neither of us had ever been to Scotland. As the horse and cart which had come to meet us clopped its way through the chilly darkness, we plied the liveried horseman with questions. Was that light in the trees the castle? How many rooms were there? Was it haunted?

At last we turned off the main road into the drive, past a turreted lodge and into a wood. At this point from out of the shadows came a series of shrieks which made the horse shy and jerk the reins, and the horseman speak for the first time.

"Some folks do say the place is fair haunted," he said slowly. "Aye, aye, but yon was an owl. Ye'll be safe enough in the castle. Ye will that." Wartime London, which included bombs from a Zeppelin, seemed a good deal safer, and as we turned a corner, there, ahead of us, suspended in the dark night, was a faintly lit vaulted arch. Another screech owl performed as the cart drew up to the house.

The horseman helped us down and as the studded door under the Tutor's arch swung open, lamplight touched the polished stem of a huge key projecting from an equally large lock. Beyond this, what seemed to be an enormous skull was hovering above my mother. It was an elephant's, and next morning when daylight drained the pools of shadow from its eye sockets, and showed the sturdy chains supporting its tusks, it became more acceptable.

There followed days of carefree adventure as my friend Leslie and I explored. When the crested keybox was opened and the rows of keys examined, each with its own label, this spoke to us of romance and the past. Which king slept in the King's Room? Who was the Fraser of the Fraser Room? Were there soldiers in the Barrack Room? Choice mystery of all was the keyless label with "key of the concealment room at north end of the trance" inscribed on the back of an old hand-painted playing card. My mother did her best to answer our endless questions from knowledge supplied by the housekeeper before (for the sake of economy) she was asked to leave, with her head in the air, and a very large amount of luggage. She was my mother's only link with the last laird, Colonel Francis Romulus Pollard-Urquhart RHA of Craigston and Castle Pollard. A widower without children, his young nephew Michael, my father, was deemed to inherit the entailed estate of Craigston.

The colonel, having groomed his heir for a career in the army, disapproved of my father running away from Sandhurst to fight the Boers and even more of his love for the girl he met while convalescing in her family's home in Natal. To him she was a "colonial", though from a well-known Gloucestershire family, and he refused to meet her. My father, having been taken prisoner and lost two toes due to a forced march to Ladysmith, was in no mood to compromise. He married Natalie and became a coffee planter in India, where I was born. The rift was irreparable.

When the colonel died the entail passed to his brother, a frail monk in Fort Augustus, who lived long enough for his Order to sell the more valuable unentailed contents of the castle, but not to pay for death duties. My mother, having the pioneer's urge to face adventure and hardship, and faith in the ownership of land, persuaded my father, still fighting in France, to accept the challenge of his inheritance and, against everyone's advice, to live in the castle.

The Great War over, Michael returned to battle with double death duties and an estate without capital. Agriculture was

Miss Eleanor Urquhart by Raeburn, *Mellon Collection, National Gallery of Art, Washington DC*

depressed, rents low, and the Bank of Scotland concerned at his mounting overdraft. It was decided to sell Raeburn's portrait of Eleanor Urquhart. She was seated so that the light fell on her fragile white muslin dress, her fair hair merging with the evening landscape behind. It was the kind of picture that Duveen knew Mellon would buy, and it is now in the Washington National Gallery. Charles Morgan, the novelist, took her as the model for his heroine in *Sparkenbroke*, and an American came every year from Washington to see where she lived, a copy of the picture in a pocket next to his heart. His name, Doty, only ceased to recur in our visitors' book when he married, not because I suggested he add another 't' to his name!

The castle remained much as Colonel Francis Pollard-Urquhart had left it, but without his staff, money or equipment. The plumbing was early Victorian, the lighting, oil lamps, and heating from open coal fires in high ceilinged rooms was minimal. The colonel had wintered in Ireland, hunting from Castle Pollard, and there are many letters from female Urquharts enjoying the sunshine in Florence or Rome. After India and stuffy boarding houses in London, the cold struck us dumb. We didn't speak about it, we kept moving. The kitchen was twenty minutes walk from the dining room, a four-windowed room with three outside walls. At least the floor was draughtproof as it had been stuffed with heather to prevent indiscreet conversation penetrating into the housekeeper's room below.

The bedrooms, apart from the servants' quarters in the south wing, spun off the two narrow spiral staircases up either side of the tower and were entered at different levels and protected by double doors. These kept their inmates well sealed off, their only means of communication being a woven silk bell-rope which could agitate one of the bells in a passage on the ground floor.

Before my father was demobilised, my mother persuaded one of his cousins and two of her friends to come and share the almost empty castle with her. One night when the wind whined round the tower, twigs falling from an old beech opposite her window woke Natalie as they scratched against the glass. Remembering that the tree was considered too close to be safe, she dressed, lit a candle and climbed the spiral staircase to a sheltered room on the leeward side of the castle, known as the Red Room. The Victorian four-poster bed, draped with heavy wine-coloured hangings, with wallpaper, curtains and carpets to match, gave her a warm sombre feeling of security and soon she began to doze. Suddenly she thought she heard voices, and wondering if she might have disturbed her guests, lit a lamp and went out in the gallery at one end of which was a guest room, and the other the entry to the secret passage. Hearing nothing more, she returned to her room. After a few minutes she began to hear the same rise and fall of voices, and then a bell tolling faintly. Thoroughly alarmed, she woke and terrified her cousin, who admitted to hearing unexplained noises, and in turn woke her friends.

They discussed the possibility of church bells and a German invasion, but an opened window failed to encourage this theory. Next morning, exhaustive enquiries produced no results other than convincing reasons on the part of the guests to return home. A few days later Rachel Grant Duff, a keen antiquarian and pre-Raphaelite, drove over from Delgaty to say that my mother's experience was exactly the same as my great-aunt Leonora's who had finally refused ever to sleep in the castle again and settled in Rome. One day a psychic Polish gentleman was brought by Rachel to identify which room in the castle might be haunted, and unhesitatingly he picked the Red Room.

Varied accounts of the ghostly sounds continued, and what with lamp-lit passages, empty rooms, and the wind moaning, rattling windows, and creaking unseen doors, my poor sister was scared out of her wits. It became difficult to keep servants and the number of guests who would spend more than one night in the castle grew fewer. I myself avoided the upper storeys after dark, and slept with a small flintlock pistol under my pillow. Perhaps for economic reasons, as my mother had started taking paying guests, the Bishop of Aberdeen came to exorcise the unhappy ghost.

As the future of Craigston continued to swing in the balance, I began to feel the chills of genteel poverty and to dread the inheritance my parents slaved for. At Oxford I began to read Modern Greats, and it was there that a lifelong interest in my ancestor, Sir Thomas Urquhart of Cromarty, began. But my father and I decided

Craigston Castle

that if we were to save the ailing castle, I should read something more technical than philosophy. So I obtained an MA in Forestry and became an Assistant Conservator in Nigeria. I might have known the tempting salary and long holidays were for something other than my degree. Three years in tropical rain forests and malaria, amoebic dysentry, and a bite from a mad dog persuaded me I was ailing faster than the castle; so I resigned and became a forestry consultant in England — a poorly paid but fascinating profession.

In 1940 my father died on active service as an Able Seaman. He was over age for the army, and I never understood how he got into the Senior Service. But how delighted he would have been to know that a Victorian Act exempted his estate from death duties and so again the castle had a chance of survival.

Demobilised, I returned to my profession, this time in Scotland, first with the Landowners Co-operative Forestry Society which I helped to turn into the Scottish Woodland Owners, and then as a private consultant on my own. I made many lifelong friends, amongst whom was the late Lord Cawdor. Apart from his forestry interests he was Chairman of the newly formed Historic Buildings Council and he urged me to apply for a grant to cover the cost of the cumulative repairs my father couldn't afford. It was in the national interest, he said, to spend relatively small sums on historical buildings before they became expensive burdens to the Exchequer, and that Craigston seemed a perfect example of the type of problem the Council was set to solve. Staying at Cawdor, I began to understand the power an ancient family possession had on its inheritors, and I could see my hope of a peaceful life in a comfortable farmhouse receding.

My wife had lived in the castle all through the war and became associated with the intimacies of its past, working among books in the library, cleaning pictures, saving bits of furniture and reading old family letters from the Charter Room. She loved it; the castle had won. So, given the green light by HBC, we called in Robert Hurd to administer the grant we were awarded. Away went the ancient ivy full of starlings' nests and rats' ladders to the first storey windows; up went the scaffolding and rose-tinted harling. After some architectural rumblings, Hurd's exposure of the massive red sandstone quoins in the friable conglomerate walls was accepted as being the Tutor's deliberate show of strength, not Victorian romanticism. In the soffit of the arch, the masons, scraping off a thin skin of lime,

Carved wooden shutters in the drawing room at Craigston, 16th century

revealed the blue tempera ribs of what was once a trompe l'oeil of a vaulted roof. This greatly excited Ancient Monuments, who believed it to be a unique example of tempera painting on stone; a few months later they put up scaffolding again so it could be preserved and photographed.

Restored, and glowing in its new finery, the castle still daunted me: so many rooms, so few inhabitants, so much to do. Then I remembered a course I had attended on adult education during the war, where I had met Mr Jones, once Lloyd George's amanuensis and the Secretary of the Pilgrim Trust. This meeting, coupled with the responsibility for the lives for some two hundred men for three years of the war sprouted the seeds of an idealism Oxford had planted in me, and perhaps I had a few wild genes from Thomas Urquhart with his dreams of a Universal Language. Also, having worked briefly in the forestry department of Darlington, I saw the beginning of Leonard Elmhirt's rural revolution. Surely with this castle I could do something for that humanising spark of curiosity which I had seen among bored men.

After much research and publicity, there began what the press called "The Craigston Community Centre". The Great Hall was cleared; a small stage erected at the north end, and the south wing converted into a canteen. Lecturers from Aberdeen University, concerts and displays from the Arts Council, films, debates and garden fêtes followed in quick succession. A weekend course for the Glasgow branch of the WEA brought industrial workers to see what farming was about. The platform given to Duncan, that remarkable agarian economist, who also happened to be the founder of the Farm Servants' Union, and the few boys who turned up occasionally with hammer and sickle badges in their buttonholes, gave us a reddish hue. However, the Queen Mother came over from Balmoral and gave the castle her blessing and the room where we entertained her is named after her.

The Department of Education refused to accept that the experiment was worthy of any special financial support, even though I offered to endow it with the gift of two farms if it would match the gift. So after five years the Centre closed and what funds we had went towards the cost of a village hall.

My role as forestry adviser took me to estates over the whole of Scotland and I often found myself like a family solicitor, a confidant of both generations, urging each to trust the other, and the kind of axe I had to grind made me many close friends. I began to believe that "heraldry and history" need not, except perhaps in the Highlands, turn one into an improvised eccentric. As time went on, my family was drawn into the romantic Jacobite world of some of our scholarly friends such as the Taylors, and the castle tightened its hold, impelling me to a place in its lineage. I began to steep myself in its history and take an interest in the 18th-century library which, but for my wife, I might have sold to pay school fees.

Sir Thomas Urquhart of Cromarty manifested a high degree of

strangeness in his writings, and a romantic passion for the Royalist cause which lost him his estate. Though never long at Craigston, he is the best-known member of the family and well chronicled. At Oxford I had discovered the wonder of his translation of Rabelais, called by J. C. Squire one of the great translations of the world, and stimulated by Cyril Wilkinson, Dean of Worcester College and a bibliophile, I became really interested in him. When Wilkinson came to stay at Craigston, loaded with presents for the children, we searched in the libarary catalogue for books which must have gone to Fort Augustus. The Rabelais which we still had, perhaps because it was not in the Index, he took to the Bodleian to see if the hand-written first page might be Sir Thomas's script. He was delighted to find the unpublished copies of George Glover's prints with Urquhart on Helicon not only with his titles, Apollo and the Muses paying homage, but a superimposed figure in the left-hand corner.

Through Mrs Clive Pearson of Parham, I met Mr Dring of Quaritch, who bid for me at Sothebys and gradually filled gaps in Sir Thomas Urquhart's shelf. Thanks to Cosmo Gordon, who had been Librarian for the Advocates Society, before he retired to Insch, we developed irregular soirées to which came Douglas Simpson, Aberdeen University Librarian, and Alec Keith of the University Press, and with a bottle or two beside a roaring fire I learnt about books. Cosmo sometimes brought prestigious bibliophiles and before he died gave me a 1593 edition of Rabelais in its original French binding. I learnt that Sir Thomas had almost certainly used Randle Cotgrave's French Dictionary for his translation and discovered how he invariably took Cotgrave's rarest synonym, adding a few of his own to catch the robust resonance of Rabelais, without worrying too much about accuracy. Our local school-mistress said she was disappointed that I told someone her pupils played Rabelaisian games. I showed her the text but without the nursemaid's endearments for Gargantua's penis, such as "my busher rusher, my coney burrow ferret". Rabelais was a physician as well as a priest, and it was his rich humour when ridiculing abuses of the church that saved him from persecution, but gave him the name for bawdiness.

On the 14th May 1639 Thomas Urquhart took the field in the first skirmish of the war in Scotland. His party of Royalists so surprised the Covenanters who occupied Turriff that they fled and the ensuing rout in which only three men were killed became known

Sir Thomas Urquhart of Cromarty

as "The Trot of Turriff". There is no record of Craigston's involvement, though situated only five miles from Turriff. It was probably because the young laird, an embryo Royalist, one day to be knighted by Charles II, was then only six years old. In the civil war that developed, it is more than likely the castle sheltered Royalists and Episcopalians in "the concealment room at the North end of the Trance".

Failure in the field, and pursued by debts largely inherited from his father, Thomas travelled to London where he was knighted by Charles I, and in 1645 published his book on trigonometry "for the benefit of those that are mathematically affected". though affectionately dedicated to his mother it is doubtful if she ever read it. We have a first edition but, alas, with no sign that it might have come from Sir Thomas's library at Cromarty.

At the age of forty, in 1651, Sir Thomas arrived at Worcester accompanied by attendants and seven large portmantles, three of them full of manuscripts in folio. The battle of Worcester took place on the 3rd September with "the total rout of the Regal party", and Sir Thomas, unharmed, was taken prisoner and "five times plundered, pillaged, pilfered, robbed and rifled". Classified as one of the privileged "persons of quality" he escaped being sold into plantation slavery and was put first in the Tower and then for a month in Windsor Castle. Whilst there, he realised his only hope of a pardon from Cromwell was to offer "out of the nimble reach and perspicacity of his wit" ideas and "literary chaffer" such as the Universal Language, and his short-cut to trigonometry based on Napier's logarithms, and the promise of inherited genius from his exceptional genealogy. Some of the manuscripts were saved from the soldiers who had "six hundred and forty two quintonions from which to choose paper for lighting pipes, inferior employments and posterior uses"; enough at least, to obtain permission to visit Cromarty, but alas, not to be pardoned by Cromwell.

He was last heard of in 1658 exiled in Holland, when he wrote challenging John Urquhart to a duel for usurping his right to Cromarty. Persecuted by his debtors, fighting for his King and for his religion, his genius unrecognised, he is said to have died in 1660 in Middleburg in a fit of laughter when told of the Restoration.

Perhaps Sir Thomas's ghost revenged him by inducing his usurping cousin's dramatic end, recorded in this family letter. "One day my daughter-in-law, Lady Jane Urquhart, sister of the Marquis of Montrose, heard groans in the dining room and found Sir John pacing about with his morning gown drawn closely about him. When she enquired about his disordered appearance, he wildly replied, 'Woman, would you see?' and throwing open his robe de chambre, displayed his breast stuck with knives and forks which had been lying on the beaufort and covered with blood. At this horrible sight she fainted away."

Perhaps too it was this ghost which caused the castle to change hands eight times in the next eighty years, until at last it was bought by Patrick Duff, the father of thirty-six children, twenty-three of them by his second wife, Mary Urquhart, the great-grand-daughter of the Tutor. In Banff one day, Patrick amiably patting the head of a small boy said, "And whose wee mannie are you?" "Och ye old fool, do ye no ken your own bairn," came the sharp reply. His enormous family seems to have been Patrick's only contribution to Craigston, though in the library exist landscapes by William Adam and plans for improvements he probably could not afford. In the Charter Room a schedule of work mentions "to put a spout for throwing water out at the nursery window".

For the Urquharts, Patrick's sale of Craigston to his brother-in-law, Captain John Urquhart, great-grandson of the Tutor, was possibly the most important event in their history. He began his adventurous life at the age of seventeen as a sailor fishing and trading across the North Sea. Like most seafarers he was religious, and in the Charter Room is his list of "Blissings and Dangers escaped thanks to God"; such as drowning at Christian Sands, and shipwreck at Zealand, both valuable experiences for his boisterous future as a merchant adventurer.

In December 1718 he wrote to James Urquhart of Meldrum with the surprising news that he hoped to join the Royal Navy, which in fact gave him a well-paid passage in an English ship solely to join the Spanish Armada, little knowing that six years later he would be fighting against Lord Grenada's squadron in which he had sailed at the siege of Gibraltar, and thanking God, he had been missed by an English cannonball. Before this engagement he had been to London enquiring about bottomry, which I was relieved to find was a nautical term for hiring a ship. As a Jacobite and an officer of the Armada he was able to obtain a licence from His Catholic Majesty to trade with the Spanish colonies and evidently raised enough money to charter three English-built ships which sailed to his HQ in Cadiz.

Captain John Urquhart of Craigston and Cromarty, *Country Life*

From there at the age of twenty-seven began his career as a merchant, borne out by bills of lading and letters to his agent and lawyers. In his twenty-one years at sea he made a fortune, enough to buy back Craigston and Cromarty. His portrait hanging in the drawing room at Craigston is said to be one of Travesani's best military paintings. The captain's visits to Italy evidently developed in him a taste for art, and he employed William Mossman, the Aberdeen painter, to purchase paintings for him from Rome, Naples and Venice; several are still in Craigston today.

In 1737 he retired from fifteen years' service at sea to marry his cousin Jean Urquhart, the seventeen-year-old heiress of Meldrum, and two years later bought Craigston from his brother-in-law, Patrick Duff, and in 1741, Cromarty with its 15th century castle. Though no longer on the Spanish Main, bills continued to be drawn on his agents in Cadiz, and his London lawyer, Cattenach, was still investing. By 1753 the castle had taken the shape it has today, and the farm buildings he designed and his son William completed in 1766 were so well planned that I was able in the early 1950s to adapt them for drying and storing five hundred tons of grain without spoiling their appearance.

In Spain Captain John had become a Roman Catholic and his letters of advice to his son reflect a kindly pious character, though an antipathy, not unlike Sir Thomas's, for Presbyterians, especially at Cromarty, which meant that he spent most of his old age at Craigston. Though he perceived the futility of the 1745 Rising, it is difficult to know how far Craigston was involved. A letter from Huntly Castle proved he gave money to the cause and confirms the captain's limited support, but another from a Hanoverian spy suggests Jacobites in the secret passage and his wife's displeasure at visitors to her kitchen. Not for the first time the clouds of civil war began to hang around the castle; political pressures built up, and women carriers from Turriff travelled, disguised as men, to report the movement of troops. The Laird, his rooms full of portraits of the Stuarts, the two Keiths, Peter the Great and other Jacobite heroes, was clearly torn between his loyalties and convinced like his friend, Duncan Forbes of Culloden, of Jacobite failure.

Four years later, when most of the structural work on the castle and its outbuildings was completed he expressed his feelings in a letter to his son William. "I recommend you to be Cautious in entering into Buildings or Repairs of houses; Architects and Drawers of Plans, misleading Gentlemen, either by their real Ignorance or designed miscalculation of the expence, which always comes out much greater than expected." Though no Chesterfield, he wrote letters full of wisdom applicable to any young laird of today. "Endeavour all you can to shun Lawpleas, which are not only very expensive but also chagreen peoples tempers and carry them from their Business to Edinburgh, which is an idle, expensive and Dangerous Town for Country Gentlemen."

William is remembered for his literary taste which created a unique 18th century library, and for a splendid chimney piece made of pink and white Islay marble in the Blue Room. His grandson, another William, infected by Victorian optimism, called in John Smith, the architect of Balmoral. Whether he had read the captain's warning or hadn't enough money, the castle escaped most of Smith's romantic extravaganza, and only the porch with its Tudor eyebrow was built.

The male line ended when my great-grandmother Mary Belle married William Pollard, an Irish M.P., of Castle Pollard, Co. Westmeath. I had the questionable pleasure of visiting Castle Pollard as a small boy, travelling through Dublin the day of Casement's execution, thrilled to see trams lying on their side in the street, and riding to Mullingar station with my mother in a cattle truck. Castle Pollard is now a lunatic asylum, and Mary Belle is commemorated by the baronial South Lodge at Craigston built in 1885.

A castle to survive two revolutions, two world wars, three hundred and eighty-two years of fire and tempest, and still shelter the family that built it, should satisfy the conservationists, and being a listed building please the antiquarian. Whether the lived-in look, and the genealogical aspect which distinguish it from the grander castles owned by the National Trust of Scotland will continue is more dicey. Without thirty-six children, or a wife with equally hardy qualities, a penchant for plumbing and a head for heights, the need for a castle diminishes. However, I believe the Tutor's home will take one of our many grandchildren as its custodian and that he or she will find the ensuing love hate relationship more tolerable than I have.

The Sobieski Stuarts

Flora Fraser

EILEAN AIGAS

For some years the Sobieski Stuarts, an eccentric pair of brothers, had been roaming the Eastern Highlands. They dressed in Napoleonic cavalry uniform or Royal Stuart tartan, and gold spurs clanked at their heels. Their faces were long and gaunt, adorned with long moustaches and waxed imperial beards. A certain resemblance to Kings of the Stuart line was heightened by the flowing locks they wore in ringlets. On enquiry, they told their story candidly enough.

They were grandsons of Bonnie Prince Charlie and of Louise of Stolberg, to whom Charles Edward was briefly married in the 1770s. Their father was born in secret in Italy and despatched to England to be brought up by a certain Admiral John Carter Allen, with the Admiral's own son, John.

Known as Thomas Allen, Charles Edward's son became a lieutenant in the navy, then resigned his commission, married and went to live in France. Here his sons John Sobieski and Charles Edward were born, here they received a superior education, unaware of their strange and noble heritage. Only in 1811 was this revealed to them. John was then sixteen, Charles Edward, twelve.

Their imaginations were set on fire by their father's revelations. Straightaway, they joined Napoleon's army, as the best way, presumably, of demonstrating their distaste for the Hanovers of England. They fought in the cavalry at Leipzig and at Dresden. Napoleon himself honoured Charles Edward when the youth tried to save a Polish general from drowning. The Emperor took the Cross of Louis from his buttonhole and pinned it to his officer's coat, remarking that he was worthy of the chivalrous race from which he sprang. At Waterloo, dressed in "dolman green, pelisse of crimson dye", the brothers fought for the last time.

Determined to fulfil their destiny, John and Charles Edward left Boulogne for London in 1818. There they applied themselves seriously to the Gaelic tongue, under the direction of an old Highlander. Armed with his new knowledge, John went north to Argyllshire and made the Highland chiefs there, the Argyll among them, acquainted with his claims. Charles Edward, meanwhile, offered a lady caught in a shower his umbrella and was soon married.

While John went abroad, Charles Edward and his Anna moved to Edinburgh, so that their child might be born a Scot. The "Countess" Marie was duly born, and her parents moved in the best Scottish circles. With the return of John from abroad in 1826, the brothers determined to settle in the Highlands.

A word must here be said of Scotland in the 1820s. All hope, or fear, of a Stuart restoration was dead, save in the brothers' breasts. Long ago, most of the rebels' lands had been restored, though often not their attaindered titles. The Lovat lands had been restored in 1774, and the Master who was "out" in the '45 reigned as M.P. for Inverness from 1761 till his death.

The reception of the brothers' claims in the Lowlands was tolerated from the lack of interest. In the Highlands the Sobieski Stuarts met with greater curiosity and were patronized cheerfully by several Highland lairds. Whether or not the brothers' claims were believed, they were entertaining company in an area where little of note occurred from year to year. In a dilatory fashion, the Earl of Moray and others supported the brothers' claim and made them free of their estates in Morayshire. Here the brothers hunted and shot; here Clementina and Sobieski joined Marie in the new generation of Stuarts.

In 1837 Lord Lovat in nearby Inverness-shire gave tangible proof of his friendship with the Sobieskis. He offered them a home anywhere they chose on his estates. The Sobieskis chose Eilean Aigas, a wooded island in the River Beauly.

The island of Aigas rises like a hedgehog with pine quills bristling from the river. Its borders are a mass of rhododendra and bracken. A Victorian bridge with stone balustrade is its only connection with the world outside — an altogether different world of farmland and cattle. At the eastern point of the island, a mossy platform some thirty feet above sheer cliffs surveys a wide basin of water and granular cliffs rough with lichen. Immediately below this point, a bare rock stands in the water and husbands two wavering saplings.

No birds nest there. Beyond the gloomy magnificence of the Gorge, boulder cliffs of the mainland bulge to meet their rocky counterparts on the northern face of the island. The southern side of the island is tranquil, with oaks and maples bordering the river which runs close at hand. In late spring, bluebells mass here among green rushy leaves and scent the damp air.

John and Charles Edward Sobieski Stuart were proficient carpenters. With their own hands they adapted the existing house and its interior to suit their own extravagant notions of what was due to them. Busts of Napoleon and of their supposed Stuart forebears jostled with silver pistols once fired by Prince Charlie. Stags' heads bore witness to their expertise on the hill, and Jacobite targes and basket-handled swords were arrayed on the walls. The palace doors they built were flung open and high-backed ceremonial chairs were set behind long trestle tables for royal feasts. They sat on a dais, lairds of the locality beneath them, and then a motley "tail" of crofters stretched from the hall, through the present drawing room and out of French windows into the honey-scented gardens beyond. If any were so foolish as to propose the King's health, Charles Edward raised his glass silently to his brother.

The Sobieski Stuarts by John Sobieski Stuart

They were called "The Long-haired Chiefs" by the crofters round about. On Sundays and holy days, the family — John and Charles Edward, Anna, the lovely Marie, Clementina and Sobieski — proceeded in stately fashion, missals in hand, to a little cove on the southern side of the island. There, a barge, decked with flowers, waited to take them two or three miles up-river to the little church of Eskadale. Devout Catholics, the Sobieskis were granted a special pew by Lord Lovat. It is said that of all the honours granted the brothers, this enraged Queen Victoria the most.

The brothers, having made their realm a lovesome thing, with gardens and walks, settled down in the room now known as the book-room, to write a great work. This was *Vestiarium Scoticum,* a classic account of Highland dress. Hunting expeditions into the glens inspired a compendium of Highland lore, *Lays of the Deer Forest*, from which this poem is taken:

"MY OWN" DARK "LAND"

Where is the autumn with her ruby light,
The roaring torrents, and the streamers bright?
Where is the eagle with his dark red wings,
The snow-white mantle, and the plume of kings?
Where the brave children of the targe and brand? —
"Far, far in my own" dark "land."

Where is the winter where the north wind blows,
The dark blue mountain and the velvet snows?
Where the dun brothers of my lonely day,
The antlered monarch, and the goshawk grey?
Where the sea chorus floating to the strand?
"Far, far in my own" dark "land." —

Where is the sun the livelong night,
Sheds on the sea the pale twilight?
Where is the hunter's glorious moon,
Lights on the heath a paler noon,
The lake of otters and the roe-tracked sand?
"Far, far in my own" dark "land."

Where is the hall where the thunders sleep,
The ocean roaring in its vortex deep?

Where the hill bowers where the sweet birch grows,
The fawns light bounding, and the slender oes?
Where the bright mermaid and her crystal cell?
"Far, far" where the north winds dwell. —

Where is the falchion by the swart elves given,
The war-pipes calling the grey hawks from heaven?
Where the bright standard with its eagle wings,
The jewelled lyre with the silver strings?
Hills of the banner, harp, and brand,
"Far, far in thy own" dark "land." —

There the white rose sheds her flower,
There the rowan spreads her bower,
There the wild swan builds her nest,
There the dun deer makes his rest —
Land of eagles, storms, and snows!
Far, far where the dark heath grows!

Beallach-a-Mhinisteir, *July 1828.*

Clementina and Sobieski, who spent their childhood here, had a circumscribed upbringing, sad to relate. Forbidden to make paper boats on the way to church, they were equally prohibited from entering their mother's or Marie's gardens. They were, however, promised a garden of their own one day. They were only allowed to walk in the grounds under supervision, and hideous penalties were allotted to ventures up to the attics.

Did the Sobieskis seriously dream of raising the Stuart standard once more in Scotland? There is a story that they heard Queen Victoria was to be present at an assembly in Edinburgh. They decided to attend, in no doubt that the usurper had but to see them and, trembling, offer them the throne. Flushed with anticipation, dressed in their finest, they waited through a long evening. Lady Eastlake in 1843 gives a description of Charles Edward: "dressed in all the extravagance of which Highland costume is capable — every kind of tag and rag, false orders, and tinsel ornaments which could be heaped on. . . ."

Long did the brothers wait for the call. Worthies of Edinburgh and other notables were called in turn to the ante-chamber where the Sovereign sat. The Sobieskis grew troubled in spirit, then heavy

Drawing of Eilean Aigas by the author at the age of eight

at heart. The Queen departed, the evening was at an end. The Sobieskis retreated to the royal trappings of their island home, but the coronets on their paperweights, the Stuart pennon on the barge, were as ash in their mouths. In 1846 they left Eilean Aigas for the Continent, much mourned by local spectators of their tartan sound and fury

The Sobieski Stuarts spent their later years earnestly researching their claim to the throne of England in the Reading Room of the British Museum at table number 6. To the delight of other readers, John Sobieski wore a long, blue cavalry coat, full honours, and, of course, his spurs.

The brothers did not forget Eilean Aigas. On his death in 1872, John Sobieski was buried in the Eskadale churchyard up-river from the island, under a Celtic cross, and in 1880, gallant Charles Edward joined his brother under the same monument. The cross still stands. weathered now; Eilean Aigas has its palace doors yet, its ceremonial chairs. Above the book-room fireplace hangs John Sobieski's exact painting of himself and his brother in full rig in that very room. Walking now from the tartan book-room, hung about with prints and early photographs of the brothers, through the drawing room and out to the heady scent of wild azaleas framing a view of the quiet river, the Sobieski Stuarts would not find Eilean Aigas so very changed.

Finis

Family Tree

George and Jane MacMillan

FINLAYSTONE

In the demi-paradise known locally as Finlaystone Gardens there stands — or, more accurately, leans — an ancient tree not far to the west of the house itself. It is not the Tree of Life. Indeed, it seems that only the deer can eat its leaves with impunity; for it is a yew. Nor could it be called a tree of knowledge: the mists of time hang densely round its branches. It has been there, or therabouts, almost as long as the house itself, according at least to tradition. Dendrologists have sometimes questioned its age; but none has staked his reputation on his scepticism, partly because the tree forks at a point well below the normal height at which trees are measured for establishing their age.

So, until it is proved wrong, we accept the strong tradition that in 1556 John Knox celebrated the first reformed Communion in the West of Scotland at or near the point where the tree stood. His patron was Alexander Cunningham, fifth Earl of Glencairn, one of the fifteen earls who held Finlaystone from the early fifteenth to the late eighteenth century.

The Earl and the Reformer were undoubtedly men of dynamism, but they seem to have been somewhat remiss in their organisation. It suddenly became apparent that they were embarking on a Communion service without one vital prop — Communion cups. Knox, in some desperation, said anything would do provided it had not been used for frivolous purposes. Even that stipulation seems to have caused problems in the Glencairn household. But at last they hit on the idea of inverting some candlesticks and drinking the wine from their hollow bases. For at least two centuries these candlesticks were kept in the house and sent up to the local parish church on Communion Sundays. Receipts were signed every time they were used but at the end of the eighteenth century they mysteriously disappeared. Some said they had been immured in the house; others, perhaps more realistically, that they had been flogged by the last Countess.

Knox's visit to Finlaystone seems to have passed off peacefully enough, but it was a rare moment of tranquillity in the turbulent story of the Glencairns — and of the Scotland in which they lived.

By the middle of the sixteenth century the Cunningham family had gained a powerful position in Scottish political life by a combination of adroit marriages and reasonably successful backing of royal favourites. Some of their bets, it is true, had gone astray. The first Earl, for example, lost his life while foolishly trying to defend James III against his usurping son at the battle of Sauchieburn in 1488. James IV's reluctance to confer the earldom on the next generation has led to confusion in the numbering of earls ever since. However, it seems that no king could manage for long without a Glencairn at court. So the next generation regained the title.

In the next couple of centuries Glencairns married daughters of the Earls of Arran, Angus, Argyll, Douglas and Lothian, with one or two uncoronetted heiresses to swell their territory. Their connections and possessions did not, on the whole, prevent them from competing with their neighbours for even more. Under a series of weak kings they conducted feuds for over two and a half centuries with the Montgomeries of North Ayrshire and with the Porterfields of Kilmacolm.

William, the fourth Earl (1540 and 1547), did his share of feuding with his neighbours; but his metier was intrigue. Indeed he spent so much time at court that he can scarcely have appeared at Finlaystone. He was sent to France to fix up the marriage of James V to Mary de Guise. Though that undoubtedly reinforced the Auld Alliance, Knox — and, presumably, the next Earl — strongly disapproved of its consequences for Scotland.

Having rigged up this liaison, William was involved in the debacle of Solway Moss (1542) when ten thousand Scots ran away from three hundred English cavalry, leaving him and his fellow-aristocrats to be captured. After a period of discomfort in England, he and his friends were released, having agreed to help Henry VIII get his hands on Scotland. His match-making experience was again enlisted — this time to pair off Mary (future Queen of Scots), still in her cradle, with the future Edward VI, soon to be in his untimely grave. He abandoned what might have been his second scoop when Henry became too grasping for his taste.

William's ardent support of the Reformation seems to have upset the Earl of Arran, who had the authority of Regent. In a subsequent battle, Glencairn lost his second son. Curiously enough, that did not prevent his heir, Alexander, from marrying Arran's daughter, who seems to have been as keen on the Reformation as any Glencairn.

Alexander, Earl from 1547 to 1576, was Knox's patron and exceptional only by virtue of the fact that his violence was not directed against his neighbours, but against the opponents of religious reform, and more particularly against idols. Three years after Knox visited Finlaystone, he preached so powerfully on idolatry to the good people of Perth that they disinherited some local friars and smashed every available statue. That annoyed the Queen Regent (Mary de Guise) and she threatened to eradicate Perth. Glencairn raised a force of about 250 horse and foot soldiers, and by marching day and night reached Perth so quickly that he foiled the impending siege. Paradoxically, he was next year rewarded by being made a Privy Councillor to the young Queen Mary. At that point his religious zeal got the better of him and he smashed up Holyrood Chapel and burnt part of Paisley Abbey. Was this a classic case of the sublimination of aggressive tendencies, for which many a Glencairn was noted?

Alexander's grandson, James, the seventh Earl (1580-1627), reverted to feuding with uncommon zest. His habitual dislike of the Porterfields flared into violence. A young Cunningham who defaulted on his rent to Porterfield took refuge at Finlaystone. The two families met at Kilmacolm parish church one Sunday in 1578. An insult resulted in a pitched battle in the churchyard, followed by a three-mile sprint for home by the Finlaystone gang. Smarting, they spent the next week or so plotting revenge, and then laid siege to Duchal Castle, the Porterfield stronghold. After a while, the Porterfields got bored and asked to discuss terms. The drawbridge was lowered; Glencairn and party went in, and promptly set about sacking the place. Two years later, when Glencairn was again on the run, he found himself asking Porterfield for a bed. Porterfield magnanimously let him in, but could not help remarking that the facilities had once been better.

James's reputation as a hothead seems to have made him a prime, though probably an undeserving, suspect in connection with the foul murder of the fourth Earl of Eglinton in 1586. The vendetta between the Cunninghams and the Montgomeries had already notched up two centuries. It took an ugly twist when three or four Cunninghams bound themselves to kill "the fattest of the Montgomeries", Hugh, the young Earl. His murder plunged the West of Scotland into a bloodbath. James, protesting total ignorance of the conspiracy, was fined a lot of money and seems to have been debarred from his five big houses, including Finlaystone, at least for a while. Royal displeasure must, however, have been short-lived, for within five years he was sitting in judgement on one of his more enterprising peers, the Earl of Gowrie, who had locked up the King and attempted to rule in his stead.

The Yew Tree

It is hard to believe that through all the turmoil of these times the John Knox tree was putting on weight, unhampered by fire or sword. By the beginning of the Civil War it had survived almost a century since it qualified for "Historic Tree" status.

The period reached its apogee in William, ninth Earl of Glencairn (1631-1664). He was involved not in local squabbles, however bloody, but in a complex national struggle; and, like many of his forebears, he took a leading role in it. It is said that many a secret meeting took place at Finlaystone during this period. If so, they were probably not so much "sub rosa" and "sub taxo".

William's performance during the Civil War resembles that of a high-wire artist. There were complications enough in England, but at least there were only two sides to choose from. In Scotland these were overlaid by allegiances to Presbyterian or Episcopalian forms of church government, and by squabbles within the nobility. Glencairn began the war by declaring for the King and Presbyterianism. That might have been due in part to his dislike for the Earl of Argyll, who favoured Presbyterianism and Parliament.

In the mid-fifties Glencairn marched north, raising an army in support of the future Charles II, with the object of making trouble for Cromwell's man in Scotland, the good General Monk. Glencairn's recruiting leaflet reads like a sermon, with frequent Old Testament quotations to prove the rightness of restoring the monarchy. His colleague, Lord Kenmure, tried a more successful tactic. His recruiting drum was a barrel of whisky, and he invited "all who would fecht for Charlie" to "come and partake of the mountain dew at their pleasure". This proved a magnet to thirsty Highlanders, but nearly cost Glencairn his life.

It is said that, on reaching Dornoch, Glencairn threw a party to mark the hand-over of his force to the King's Commander-in-Chief, General Middleton. At the party he waxed somewhat lyrical about the quality of his troops and was unduly put out when Sir George Munro (who may well have seen how they were recruited) dared suggest that they were "no other than a pack of thieves and robbers". There followed a duel, first with pistols on horseback (predictably, no contact) and then, more seriously, on foot, from which Sir George emerged with a cut over one eye, and the referee intervened.

Thereupon, Glencairn left for home; and his force followed his example, encouraged by the approach of General Monk. As he journeyed he fell ill in Colquhoun country, and took time off at Ross Dhu. Just to prove his fitness, he led a lunchtime swoop on Dumbarton, where he killed thirty Roundhead supporters. That could explain why we next find him locked up in Edinburgh Castle and specially exempted from a Parliamentary amnesty. He was on the point of execution when Charles II was restored, and Glencairn became Chancellor of Scotland instead.

He took full advantage of the chance to recoup his fortunes, which had reached zero. By now, he had had to choose between Kirk and King, and had opted for King. But the thought of the Presbyterian tree in his garden may well have made him drag his feet in persecuting the Presbies; for it is said that he died of an illness induced by Archbishop Sharp's reproaches on that score. Although his marital irregularities had got him into trouble with his minister, and although he had brought about the eviction of many a minister from his parish, on his deathbed he sent for Presbyterian ministers. When that was reported at court, the Duke of York remarked that, "Scotsmen, be what they would in their lives, were all Presbyterians at their death". Unlike Sharp, Glencairn died in his bed and was buried with great pomp in the national shrine of St Giles.

The next three or four earls may well have been as gifted as William, but times were quieter. Where they had spread havoc in Dumbarton, they simply governed the castle. One of them is said to have used carrier pigeons to send messages across the river to his wife back at Finlaystone. Another wrote to the Duke of Marlborough that the armoury consisted of some "olde russty bulletts and matchs". The pigeon that brought the Duke's reply must have been brought down by some better-equipped English marksman — if it was ever despatched.

Sketch of Finlaystone, *Harriet Ellis*

In about 1750 the John Knox tree suffered what may have been its first major change of habitat. From an early sketch on the margin of a map it looks as if the tree stood at the north-west corner of a tower-like house which had low wings running north and south from it. These wings were replaced by three-storey extensions on either side of the original house, which gave it a plain but recognisable eighteenth-century facade. The northern extensions must have come within yards of the tree.

Not long after this radical alteration, James, fourteenth Earl of Glencairn (1715-1791), entertained another of Finlaystone's distinguished visitors, Robert Burns. As if to refute those who claim that Burns country runs no further north than Ayrshire, Burns scratched his name with a diamond ring on a window pane as evidence of his presence. For good measure, he added the date of the bottle that he and the Earl were drinking.

This was no chance encounter, because Burns regarded the Earl as his "one true patron" — and with some justice. Glencairn owned most of the Burns country; and it was his factor, Mr Dalziel, who first brought Burns to his attention.

Unfortunately for Burns, the Earl's constitution was not as robust as those of some of his forebears. He died of pneumonia in Falmouth in 1791. Burns met this serious emotional and financial blow with a lengthy and rather conventional lament in which he compared himself with a forest tree that had outlasted most of its fellows — and certainly the best of them. He ends with the wish that the fatal blow had struck him first.

Why did I live to see the day,
A day to me so full of woe?
O, had I met the mortal shaft
Which laid my benefactor low!

The bridegroom may forget the bride
Was made his wedded wife yestreen;
The monarch may forget the crown
That on his head an hour has been;

The mother may forget the child
That smiles sae sweetly on her knee;
But I'll remember thee, Glencairn,
And a' thou hast done for me!

This last verse is said to have been a favourite quotation with Abraham Lincoln.

Even before the Earl's death, the straight-talking son of the Ayrshire soil had also turned to the Countess for support, both moral and financial.

My Lady . . .

. . . When I am tempted to do anything improper, I dare not, because I look on myself as accountable to your ladyship and family. Now and then, when I have the honour to be called to the tables of the great, if I happen to meet with any mortification from the stately stupidity of self-sufficient squires or the luxurious insolence of upstart nabobs, I get above the creatures by calling to remembrance that I am patronised by the noble house of Glencairn; and at gala times . . . when my punch-bowl is brought from its dusty corner . . . I begin with "The Countess of Glencairn". . . .

One can't help wondering what Knox would have made of this, coming from one who had more than once faced the discipline of the Kirk Session for various improprieties.

When the fifteenth and last Earl died in 1796, the estate passed to his cousin, Robert Graham of Gartmore; and a dark age descended on Finlaystone. Gambling, which had caused some trouble before, now caused havoc. William Cunninghame-Graham fell into the bad company of the Prince Regent and seems to have lost most of his inheritance. It's said that he rewarded a crony who produced £1,000 of aid one evening with the use of Finlaystone for the rest of his life. According to tradition, that life lasted another thirty years.

For most of the 1850s that remarkable late-Victorian eccentric, Don Roberto Cunningham-Graham, spent his boyhood at Finlaystone. It was, indirectly, his great-grandfather's financial mismanagement that made it necessary for him to seek his fortune abroad. But he was not compelled to conduct wagon trains in Texas or become a gaucho in the Argentine. Having survived that, and much more besides, he settled down into a seat at Westminster, where he played Benn to Gladstone's Kinnock. When not sewing mailbags in Pentonville for alleged breach of the peace, he was taking food to starving Moroccans, or riding the pampas of South America.

In about 1865 Finlaystone was rented and later bought by the chairman of the first steamship company in the world, the Clyde

Shipping Company. George Jardine Kidston spent a fortune on the garden and the house — particularly the interior.

Anyone approaching the house today must conclude that plumbing was regarded as a high priority. Every downpipe is surmounted by a box bearing the date 1900. Though it is not so obvious to the approaching guest, the one-storey moustache running along the face of the house conceals two washroom-lavatories and not much else.

The gloom cast by this excrescence on the ground floor of the house may well have compelled the architect to introduce one of his most impressive features in order to increase the daylight. To support what was once the north wall of the house, he raised two large marble pillars. If, as tradition asserts, he brought them in through the front door, that was itself a triumph of engineering. But, as usual, we have no record of this or any other interior alteration.

We do, however, have photographic proof of the moving of the John Knox tree.

It should be explained that George Kidston's wife had died young, after giving birth to nine children. His considerable household was run by his sister, Miss Hamilton Campbell Kidston. He could not afford to lose her.

Miss Hamilton Campbell Kidston (or Aunty Bye, as her brother's children more succinctly called her) was a keen embroidress. As the house was being turned inside out, she took her opportunity and hinted that she could do with a better light to sew by. Her brother was not slow to respond. Why he threw out the bow window where he did is not quite clear. He was, of course, in the hands of the architect Sir John James Burnett, a contemporary of Charles Rennie Mackintosh. A bow window thrown anywhere else would certainly have looked odd. All the same, it's hard to believe that it was not until the window was complete that Mr Kidston realised that John Knox's tree was in the light.

It seems that even in 1900 the tree preservationist lobby was active; or else Mr Kidston had a strong sense of history himself. He certainly seems to have had a healthy respect for timber. It is said that he was only once in his life seen to be really angry, and that was when he found some of his children shortening the legs of his drawing room chairs with the aid of a saw. At all events, he was most reluctant to fell the offending tree. The only alternative was to move

The moving of the John Knox Tree in 1900.

it. But no one in Britain seemed keen to transplant a tree that had supposedly survived nearly three and a half centuries — more, if it had been big enough for Knox to do anything under it.

At last an American firm did the job, as the photographs show. Thanks to a trench, some railway lines and a team of horses, it now grows about forty yards south-west of where it stood in 1899. In 1942 Hitler tried to rectify its easterly list by dropping a bomb about fifty yards to the south-east; but he failed to make much impression. Recently, it has developed a brown patch at its crown, enough to remind us that even the days of a tree are numbered.

George Kidston's will was surprisingly unconventional. He divided his estate into thirteen notional shares, and left three of them to his eldest son, two each to his other sons, and one to each of his six daughters. The estate was preserved from dissolution when Lilian married a rich Irishman and bought out her brothers' and sisters' shares. Thereafter, Richard and Lilian Blakiston-Houston tended to spend spring and summer in Northern Ireland and autumn and winter in Scotland. Peaches from the Finlaystone greenhouses were sent across the Irish Sea in cottonwool for their delectation.

During one of their absences towards the end of the First World War, a much-admired feature of the garden sprang unauthorised into being. Photographs show that from 1900, when the gardens were laid out, the rose garden was surrounded by a yew hedge whose horizontal profile was only occasionally broken by pointed pillars. The effect was a bit dull. A relative gave Mrs Blakiston-Houston a watercolour of the castellated wall that separates Marlborough House from the Mall in London, and may even have suggested that it might serve as a model for the hedge. The sketch lay on the piano in the drawing room and nothing happened.

While Mrs Houston was away for three weeks in 1916, she left behind a French sister-in-law and her daughter's governess, both women of resource and determination. As soon as she was gone, the conspirators swung into action. To carve up sixty yards of yew hedge to resemble regular castellations requires both skill in measurement and strength of wrist. By the twentieth day they still had a few yards to go, and it was pouring with rain. Undeterred, they stuck a carriage umbrella in the hedge and worked underneath it. They must have felt great pride of achievement as they went to bed that night.

The turreted yew hedge.

Unfortunately, it was not the precision and symmetry of their work that impressed the returning mistress/hostess so much as the total lack of greenness in the hedge. She was not best pleased at the time. But she was never one to nurse a grudge. Twenty years on, when the army of gardeners had again gone to war, she and the governess were tending the hedge in perfect harmony.

The army of gardeners, having departed in 1939, never returned. Their place was taken a little while after the war by a veteran of both wars, General Sir Gordon MacMillan, who had married Mrs Houston's daughter, the girl with the governess and the French aunt.

But what of the John Knox tree now? How has it fared since its move? In spite of the brown patch at its crown — the arboreal equivalent of balding, perhaps — it seems well enough.

The coming of the Clan MacMillan — General Sir Gordon is its Chief — to Finlaystone has given the story of John Knox's tree an unexpected twist. Transatlantic MacMillans — many of them keen Presbyterians — have taken some of the rare cuttings of the tree home with them. No doubt at this very moment new legends are being born, which will reach their full maturity in four centuries' time.

The Kinloch Affair

Harriet Kinloch

GILMERTON

Gilmerton House stands in several thousand acres of prime arable land in one of the most attractive parts of East Lothian, not far from the market and county town of Haddington. Now an imposing Georgian house with some fifty rooms and set in extensive gardens, it has undergone several stages of development. The original building was knocked down in the early 17th century and in its place what is now the west wing of the house was built. In 1730 the main south-facing part was constructed to an Adam design and in 1828 the east wing was built and a porch and balcony added on to the front.

In 1655 it was purchased by Francis Kinloch, a man of wealth and influence, a burgess, MP and in 1677 Lord Provost of Edinburgh. In 1686 he was knighted for lending £300 to James, Duke of York, to enable him to travel extensively in Scotland. Thus was founded the Baronetcy of Kinloch of Gilmerton.

It was with the death in 1795 of the fifth Baronet, Sir David Kinloch, that events in the family hurtled them into the public eye in less than happy fashion. Sir David, a writer, had married Harriet, a daughter of Sir Archibald Cockburn of Langton, and they had eight children, five sons and three daughters. At the time of Sir David's death in February of that year, only Sir Francis, his heir, a brother Alexander, and a sister Janet remained at Gilmerton although the second brother, Archibald-Gordon, was a frequent visitor. Two months after Sir Francis had succeeded to the title, the tragedy occurred.

The High Court in Edinburgh opened on Monday, 29th June 1795, at 10 o'clock before the Lord Justice Clerk and the four Law Lords, Eskgrove, Dunsinnan, Swinton and Craig. The Prosecution for the Crown was represented by four lawyers led by Robert Dundas of Arniston, and four for the defence by David Hume. There was a jury of fiteen men from Edinburgh and its environs, the chairman of which was Andrew Wauchope of Niddry Marischal.

The indictment was read to the effect that Sir Archibald-Gordon Kinloch, 7th Baronet of Gilmerton, then a prisoner in the Tolbooth of Edinburgh, was accused of the murder of his brother Sir Francis Kinloch, 6th Baronet of Gilmerton, at Gilmerton House in the Parish of Athelstaneford and County of Haddington, on the night of the 14th or early in the morning of 15th April 1795. It stated that Sir Archibald left his bedroom with two loaded pistols concealed on him, and went down to the dining room where Sir Francis was. He then left the room followed by Sir Francis and on the stairs Sir Archibald "did then and there murder the said Sir Francis Kinloch, your brother by wickedly and feloniously discharging one of the said loaded pistols at your said brother, by which he received a mortal wound, the ball having penetrated below the point of the sternum or breast bone, towards the right side: And the said Sir Francis Kinloch having languished in great pain till the evening of the 16th of the said month of April, did then expire in consequence of the wound given him by you the said Archibald-Gordon Kinloch, and notwithstanding every medical assistance having been procured . . . All of which, or part thereof, being found proven by the verdict of an Assize, before the Lord Justice General, Lord Justice Clerk and Lords Commissioners of Justiciary, You the Said Sir Archibald-Gordon Kinloch ought to be punished with the pains of law, to deter others from committing the like crimes in all times coming."

So began the trial which lasted until 7 o'clock the following morning, twenty-one hours and twenty or so witnesses later. The transcript of the trial contains some 45,000 words of submissions, evidence and concluding speeches. Such an event at that time had caused a great deal of comment in the country. A highly respected family had been brought into the public gaze in a most dramatic manner. Reports and rumours were rife before the trial opened, and on the day before, Sir Archibald was even pilloried from the pulpit "the seat itself of truth and of charity", and all condemned the man in contemptuous and inhumane terms.

With this background and the bare details of the indictment laid before the court the prisoner was asked to plead. He pleaded not guilty. A paradoxical plea in view of the incontrovertible evidence of the indictment, but then Mr David Hume, advocate for the defendant, addressed the court and asked them to set aside all that they had heard of rumours and scandalmongering. "I say I am not ignorant of these reports, and of the weight of prejudice and suspicion, with which, in consequence, I have to struggle: Nor indeed with your Lordships, whose breasts are void of every feeling of the sort, and who will listen to nothing but the information of the law, and the still voice of your own conscience; but with the people at large, from among whom the persons, who as jurymen are to decide on the pannel's fate, are and must be taken. Nor My Lord, do I think it very wonderful, that such should be their feelings on this extraordinary occasion."

Mr Hume asked their careful consideration of that which was to prove a very controversial plea and one which is known to be one of the earliest recorded defences on the grounds of insanity. He then outlined the facts in the baldest terms in order to highlight the reality of the tragedy. Sir Francis, a man in his prime, who had just inherited his title, "A good and estimable person surrounded with all the fair prospects of a long and happy and a useful life", had been foully murdered under his own roof, almost at his own table amongst friends and family and by his own brother. No wonder that when the story was related it was at first heard "with a close heart and an unfavourable ear".

The address continued to the point where Mr Hume sought the court to try calmly and impartially the manner of the tragedy. He asked them to consider "whether it was chance or design, and to decide on the life and death of a frail and infirm mortal like themselves, who, if, by the will of Providence he has truly been visited with this grievous and sore affliction, and has been the instrument of destroying a brother, who never did him harm, and whom he never regarded but as a brother, is himself far more to be pitied than the deceased, and is no object of judgement, but for that Almighty Judge whose hand hath smitten him. . . ."

Mr Hume then almost tentatively came to the subject of the prisoner's defence of madness and maintained that the court could only sustain this as a relevant and lawful defence. However, he could only state the facts of the case and would not be expected to discourse on the subject of madness or attempt to ascertain "the peculiar class and character of the distemper to which this unhappy man was liable".

It was clear that it was no sudden and unaccountable fit of frenzy only manifest at the time of the murder which had been responsible for his deed. For other factors in Sir Archibald's past were found to be relevant to the case.

Fifteen years previously in 1779, Sir Archibald was serving as an army officer in the West Indies when he contracted some form of tropical fever which was then prevalent. Out of the garrison of some 5,000 men serving on St Lucia, 1,800 of them died from this virulent illness. The evidence of a Colonel Twentyman, a fellow officer, given later in the trial, supported the high opinion in which Sir Archibald was held before his illness and the colonel also graphically described the "most malignant fever, which deprived him of his senses. I had seen him in his bed in the highest state of delirium, held down in his cot by a soldier on each side, and, to use a common phrase, raving mad". A servant of Sir Archibald's also fell ill during a subsequent journey to Barbados to convalesce, and whilst in the throes of the fever simply threw himself overboard and drowned. On his return home Sir Archibald, formerly cheerful, good humoured and sociable, had become sullen, jealous and irascible. "Not only, My Lord, was there a great alteration of the temper and humour of the man, not only was there a decay of the vigour of his intellect, a confusion, weakness and cloudiness of understanding; but at times there had come to be a plain derangement and disorder — and this to such a degree as had on one occasion tempted him to turn his hand against his own life, (as he is now charged to have done against his brother's) and this an attempt of so violent and serious a nature (by cutting himself very deeply in the wrist) as occasioned him a confinement of three months, before he was again fit to come abroad."

This had been his state of health for years and more recently it had been getting worse. Plans had been made immediately before the tragedy to confine Sir Archibald in a straitjacket and keep him as a lunatic from leaving the house, but this plan had been fatally postponed. Mr Hume concluded his address having presented a plea which stood in no need of case books or precedents and commended it to the court to judge favourably, with reason and humanity.

The court then delivered their opinion and concurred with the defence plea. The jury was called and Crown evidence began. The witnesses were drawn from a cross-section of the community:

friends, servants and those involved at the time of the murder, also army colleagues of Sir Archibald who were called upon to give witness to his character. As far as can be ascertained, those staying at Gilmerton on the fateful night were Sir Francis, his other brothers Archibald and Alexander, his sister Janet, a Mr Lowe there on business and Mr Duncan McMillan, a friend and lawyer of the family who was called as the first witness.

Details of Sir Archibald's actions and behaviour immediately prior to the murder began to emerge. On Monday 13th April, Mr McMillan, accompanied by Mr Alexander Kinloch, met a chaise near Haddington as they were coming from Edinburgh. In it they recognised Sir Archibald who was obviously at pains to avoid seeing them and continued his journey towards Edinburgh. The two then dined in Haddington with Mr George Somner, the Kinloch family surgeon. During this time Sir Archibald was seen to return to Haddington and call at the Somner's shop there. He was persuaded to join them and being in such apparent mental and physical distress that they had to help him to take refreshment. They then set out for Gilmerton in two chaises, Mr Somner following with Sir Archibald in the second, thinking to get him home and out of harm's way. On the way there Sir Archibald made an excuse to stop and left the chaise to go back down the road to Haddington; one of the drivers who gave chase returned to say that Sir Archibald had said he would be in Haddington if anyone wanted him. The remainder of the party went on ot Gilmerton and stayed there for the night.

The following morning, the Tuesday, Mr Somner and Mr McMillan went to Haddington to find Sir Archibald, but without success and Mr McMillan later returned to Gilmerton for dinner. After dinner, Mr McMillan received a message from William Reid, the gardener, to say Sir Archibald had turned up at the neighbouring farm of Beanston, tenanted by Mr John Walker. Reid had gone to investigate and found Sir Archibald in a "very disagreeable situation indeed", and that he was armed with a pistol. Mr McMillan was informing Sir Francis about this just as Sir Archibald arrived at Gilmerton. He appeared to be far calmer than when earlier seen in Haddington, and retired to his room. Later that evening Mr Somner joined them at about 10 or 11 o'clock for supper which lasted until 3 o'cock in the morning, not long before the murder took place. Mr McMillan had then retired and advised the others to do so too.

During the course of Mr McMillan's evidence he was questioned about Sir Archibald's conduct generally, which he agreed was erratic and also about any disagreements there might have been between the brothers. There had been some but of no lasting significance. Sir Archibald was wont to come and go from Gilmerton very suddenly and as far as Mr Mcmillan knew no steps had been taken to confine him before the murder. It was also established that when seen in Haddington on the Monday his demeanour was not of drunkenness but of madness. Mr McMillan could not commit himself as to whether or not Sir Archibald was able to discern the difference between moral good and evil or to know that murder was a crime, a question which was to be asked of many during the trial and to which the response was invariably similar.

Mr George Somner's evidence then followed, much of which reiterated those few days' events. He had, in the recent past, been consulting doctors in Edinburgh for the family with regard to helping them cope with Sir Archibald, whom he, as a doctor, considered quite mad even though he had only limited experience of mad people. The reason for Mr Somner's presence at Gilmerton on the Tuesday night was that he had been sent for urgently by Mr McMillan and was to go there prepared. Accordingly, Mr Somner had taken a straitjacket and a nurse who had experience of caring for the insane. On arriving at Gilmerton, Mr Somner had found Sir Archibald quite quiet but still "wild looking". A discussion with Sir

Pencil drawing of Gilmerton showing front of house, *Jonathan Gibbs*

Francis followed when it was agreed that Sir Archibald should be secured, but a general unwillingness amongst the servants left the matter temporarily unresolved. Mr Somner was then examined at length on his opinion of the prisoner's madness and capacity to judge between good and evil. He was as equivocal as Mr McMillan, nor could he instance any previous family history of insanity.

The servants at Gilmerton then gave evidence most of which concerned the night of the murder and this was followed by that of doctors and lawyers who were examined on family matters which might have had a bearing on any family dispute. No possibility of this was in fact proved, but it all served to highlight the very disturbed state of Sir Archibald's mind. Three army officers provided exculpatory proof for Sir Archibald, all without exception having had nothing but the highest regard for him during his service in the army. They bore equal witness to his marked change of character subsequent to his illness in the West Indies.

Friends, colleagues and professional men had, through their evidence, built up a vivid portrait of Sir Archibald and with the evidence of his sister Miss Janet Kinloch (which in the event was curtailed as the court would not accept her giving evidence solely from notes she had written), the situation as it affected the close family became apparent, also their concern for their brother and their acceptance of eventually having to confine Sir Archibald whose behaviour had provoked Sir Francis at one time to comment, "That poor mad creature Gordon, is much raised at present, and I am afraid that one day he will be in a state of confinement."

With the evidence of Mr John Walker of Beanston Farm there was a return to the events of Tuesday, 14th April, when Sir Archibald had gone there. Mr Walker had found him walking near the house at about 5 o'clock in the morning exhausted, dishevelled and confused. Walker took him into his house and persuaded him to rest. Twelve hours later he became alarmed that Sir Archibald had not reappeared and went to rouse him. Sir Archibald partially opened the door which he had barricaded with two chairs and was seen to be holding two pistols and looking very dangerous. In an agitated state he kept pointing the guns at himself, at his heart and head and ranting all the while. Walker left him to make some tea which he then took up having first sent for Reid the gardener. Sir Archibald then started to threaten him with the pistols. Reid arrived and went up to Sir Archibald after Walker had asked him to "tell Sir Francis to send all the men in Gilmerton to Seize him, for he would do mischief either to himself or somebody else". Reid was also confronted by the pistols and in spite of Sir Archibald's reassurances that he would not be hurt he left him there and went back to Gilmerton.

In John Walker's words, "The Major came down stairs soon after, and said 'John you must give me a convoy'. I went out with him but we had not gone far when passing by the stack yard he said 'John, there was my bed among the stacks last night'. I answered 'While there was a bed in my house I am sure you had no occasion to lie there'. He desired me to walk before him but hearing him cock a pistol at my back I was alarmed, and turned about. He said 'Are you afraid John', I replied, 'No, I am sure, I have no reason to be afraid of Major Gordon'. Soon after, I heard him let the pistol down to half-cock and in a little while I heard him cock it again and in this manner we walked on together, the Major keeping behind me with the pistol. I now began to look about for an opportunity to escape, but finding I could not safely get away I went on until we came to a walk which I knew the Major was fond of. There I took my leave of him under some pretence and returned home very happy to have escaped as I did."

It was after this incident that Sir Archibald returned to Gilmerton, at the very moment when Mr McMillan was informing Sir Francis that Reid had found Sir Archibald at Beanston.

Mr Alexander Kinloch was not called upon to give evidence at his brother's trial but the dramatic events which then ensued can be taken from notes he wrote shortly afterwards, which depict better than any transcript those moments. The writer refers to himself as A.K.

"I returned to Gilmerton about three in the afternoon, there I found Miss Kinloch, Sir Francis, and a Mr Lowe from Berwickshire, for whom Sir Francis had sent to look through his lands of Athelstaneford advertised to be let by the late Sir David Kinloch. They had just dined and were drinking a glass of strong ale, a bottle of Port wine was also on the table.

"A.K. remembers dining on part of a roast fowl with some bacon and greens soon after Sir Francis being called out of the room, he entered into conversation with Mr Lowe, and to the best of his belief does not think they had conversed full half an hour when, looking round from the parlour window, he observed Major Gordon coming down the lawn before the house on the footpath leading both to the farmyard and gardens, approaching them in a most disordered state. A.K. then ran into the marble hall to look for his brother Sir Francis whom he met as he entered the hall and who had also observed the Major coming. A.K. will not be positive whether he said to his brother, 'Quickly, we must seize him', or, 'He must be seized' or 'Strong measures must be taken', but rather thinks he did then make use of such terms. Upon opening the hall door the Major advanced, clasping his hands together, looking up to heaven and addressing Sir Francis, 'Do me justice, do me justice'. At that moment Sir Francis took him by one hand as did A.K. by the other, entreated him to go to his room which he seemed averse to do and always shrank back towards the door.

"At last, quite spent with fatigue, he seemingly sunk down on the marble floor and A.K. observing a number of servants all round thinks, nay is pretty positive, that at that time he unloosened his hold from the Major's hand, crying out to those around 'Seize him' and went towards the great stair leading to the great room, in the persuasion the servants would then seize him and thinks from the helpless state he then appeared to be in, and by sinking towards the floor, that any two able bodied men could then have secured him without running any great risque of danger even supposing him armed at the time which A.K. was then ignorant of. Returning however, shortly afterwards into the dining palrour, he learnt that the Major had not been secured but that he had gone into his room and that two of the servants were with him, but who they were I do not recollect. A.K. remembers after this going into Miss Kinloch's room where his sister appeared, with her maid Helen Wells, much agitated fearing lest Major Gordon should break into her room. They bolted the door and I advised if he came rapping at the door to make no answer. He accordingly came and rapped several times at the door and no answer being made went away muttering 'Well I see I am now thrown off', or words to that purpose.

"A.K. thinks he remained with his sister and her maid for some considerable time, perhaps near two hours when the Major seemed more quiet and composed when remaining in his own room. A.K. then went down to the parlour when he remembers the Major sending for some wine and water which was made weak and sent to him. After this he repeatedly sent for Sir Francis to his room and spoke to him for a considerable length of time. Major Gordon also sent for A.K. to his room who went and when there talked, he then left him wishing him good night and a good sleep.

"About 9 o'clock in the evening, Mr George Somner came and brought with him a strait waistcoat and a woman from Haddington accustomed to attend people when insane. Many plans were talked of for seizing the Major and Sir Francis called into the house many of the servants for the purpose of seizing him. For some time the Major remained in his room and the family, betwixt 10 and 11 o'clock, went to supper. He then sent for Sir Francis and complaining much of bile in his stomach and pain in his bowels, Sir Francis unwarily gave him some pills which at the time, tho meant to give ease, might tend to increase the heat of his blood. Sir Francis, Mr Somner and A.K. resolved to sit up and see whether the Major would drop asleep or, if he was still outrageous, to endeavour to secure him and put on the strait waistcoat. A.K. remembers proposing that a letter should be wrote and delivered to him and that whilst in the act of reading, two or three people should spring upon him, seize his arms, another search his pockets for arms, and to overpower him with numbers and put on the strait waistcoat. This plan, however, was not carried out.

"After Miss Kinloch had gone to bed and Mr McMllan had retired also, Mr Somner and A.K. were sitting near the fire drinking a glass of strong ale, Sir Francis was walking up and down in the parlour and taking a glass occasionally with them. At about one or two o'clock in the morning the Major came downstairs complaining violently of the pills he had taken which Sir Francis told him 'were perfectly innocent and that he often took them himself and that when they began to operate he would find himself much relieved'. With a considerable degree of entreaty he was prevailed upon to go again to his room but shortly after he came down again with no other clothes on him but his breeches and a large great coat. For the second time that night he was prevailed upon to go to his room with great importunity. Then Sir Francis and A.K. agreed if nobody else would step forward they would seize his hands, provided the servants would come forward instantly to their assistance, and throw him down so that the strait waistcoat might be put on him.

"Several of the servants were accordingly placed in the stone parlour immediately adjoining the dining parlour. A.K. declares that during the two times the Major came into the dining parlour as before mentioned, he had not the smallest idea he, the Major, had

Archibald-Gordon Kinloch, *photograph Jessie Ann Mathews*

arms upon him, having no clothes on him except breeches and great coat. Nor did Sir Francis intimate to him his suspicion of his being armed. The fatal third time the Major came down stairs, whether he observed our countenances were more determined or from what other cause if not, but he retreated so, on towards the stair leading towards the bedrooms. Sir Francis and A.K. advanced as if persuading him to go to bed, and almost at the same moment when the Major was ascending the third or fourth step of the stair, they each seized one of his arms. A.K. thinks it was the left wrist he seized when standing on a step lower than the Major, and is confident he gripped his hand as fast that he could not put it to his body. Sir Francis, who was standing on the step of the stair above the Major, unfortunately only seized the other wrist with one hand and placed the other hand upon his shoulder so that not having entirely secured

Sir Francis Kinloch, *photograph Jessie Ann Mathews*

the hand next to him, the Major drew from under his great coat a small pistol which he fired, and the shot unfortunately took place in the body of Sir Francis, about the lower part of the belly."

The servants then immediately rushed upon Sir Archibald and dragged him down the stairs, threw him to the floor and he was secured, too late, in the straitjacket. The next morning he was taken to Haddington jail while his brother lay mortally wounded, to die in a matter of days. He was kept at Haddington until transferred to the Tolbooth in Edinburgh to await trial. During this time his health seemed to improve, perhaps as a result of being isolated from the pressures of the outside world, but he always maintained that his recollection of the murder was very indistinct. He remembered firing a pistol but not at whom and only being in the throes of insanity.

Pen and ink sketch of Gilmerton from the side, *Jonathan Gibbs*.

The rest of the trial was, predictably, much concerned with the nature and degree of insanity and Sir Archibald's insanity in particular, a subject in those times which suffered much at the hands of the law, from great loquacity, quotations from the tracts of learned people of both the medical and legal profession and lacked any firm resolution. The jury were left to reach their verdict after the Lord Justice Clerk's final words to them which were as ambivalent in the circumstances, as any of the evidence heard that day. "Gentlemen, I shall not take up more of your time. You will consider the evidence well, and decide according to your consciences. If you are convinced that he knew right from wrong, you will return a verdict of guilty. On the other hand, if it shall appear to you that he was not able to distinguish between moral good and evil, you are bound to acquit him. But Gentlemen, I think that, in all events, a verdict of not guilty is not the proper verdict for you to return. I think you ought to return a special verdict finding that the pannel was guilty of taking the life of his brother, but finding also that he was insane at the time."

On Tuesday morning, the 30th June, the jury returned their verdict after thirty-five minutes' consideration, to the effect that Sir Archibald had unanimously been found guilty of the murder of Sir Francis as stated in the terms of the indictment, but found it proved that at the time Sir Archibald was insane and deprived of reason. The court met again finally on the 15th July of that year to bring judgement to the case. The Law Lords all concurred with the jury's verdict but also perceived the necessity of preventing history repeating itself.

The final judgement was that Sir Archibald was to be taken back to the Tolbooth of Edinburgh and to remain there for his lifetime or until such a time as he could be put into the care of someone who could secure and confine him in safe custody for life, and under a penalty of £10,000 Sterling.

Following the trial, it can be assumed that Sir Archibald was indeed released into the care of his family. Knowing only the date and place of his death, 24th October 1800, at a Greenlaw House, efforts have been made to account for the last five years of his life and to find his burial place.

It was at first thought that in the absence of a marked grave in the Kinloch burial grounds either at Athelstaneford or Greyfriars in Edinburgh, Sir Archibald had most probably been kept far removed from Gilmerton and had died in ignominy. No evidence was found in the Parish records or graveyard of Greenlaw Church in Berwickshire, nor was there a Greenlaw House in the area. However, further examination of the family papers did not sustain these theories. Accounts for the years 1795-1802 were found and these gradually revealed that journeys had been made by lawyers and doctors until 1800 to a Darnhall, near Eddleston in Peeblesshire, which the Kinlochs had rented and where, in fact, Sir Archibald lived in some luxury. Accounts were found for tailors, hosiers, shoe and wig makers, booksellers and wine merchants, the latter being the most substantial items of all. He was paid a monthly allowance by his trustees of five guineas, but in whose care has not been ascertained. There was also a Minute dated 1st November 1800 which related to Sir Archibald's possessions at Greenlaw which had been sealed up there after his death. Apart from a quantity of money, valuables and more mundane items, there were four parcels of letters from members of his family which showed that he was not neglected by them over those years.

Sir Archibald's transfer from Darnhall to Greenlaw took place in July 1800. Thereafter accounts all referred to Greenlaw including a payment of window tax to Midlothian Council, but again there was no evidence to be found of such a house in Midlothian. Finally it was traced to Kirkcudbrightshire, a large house now burnt down, just north of Castle Douglas, and given the relative costs of travel then, as listed in the accounts, even at that distance from Edinburgh it seemed feasible. A return to Parish records revealed that none were kept in that area of deaths at that time and eventually an impromptu search of the records for Greyfriars Church in Edinburgh proved positive. Sir Archibald was buried there on 30th October 1800, six days after his death. The details on the Kinloch tomb which has not been used since that time are now almost obscured. There remains only the epitaph in Latin, of Magdalene McMath, the wife of the first Baronet, Sir Francis, who was buried there in 1674.

Sir Archibald, having been taken from Greenlaw House to Edinburgh, was given a full and formal funeral attended by family, friends and servants alike. Not the funeral of a sick, isolated and rejected man at all.

Gilmerton House remains today as it was then. The marble hall, the parlour now a dining room, the stone parlour now a pantry and the great staircase, scene of that tragedy, are all there, as are the Kinlochs of Gilmerton, landowners and farmers and living in greater tranquillity than their forebears.

Uncle Doddie and All

Mary Welfare

HADDO HOUSE

Haddo House has belonged to the Gordons as far back as 1469. It is situated on the lands around Methlick, a small village on the River Eltham, some twenty miles north-west of Aberdeen. But for the Covenanters, the house itself might never have existed. In 1644 Sir John Gordon was living in what was then the House of Kellie. Two years before this he had been rewarded with a baronetcy for supporting the Royalists. Soon he was to discover the dangers of such loyalty. One night, a party of Covenanters rode out from Aberdeen, burned down the House of Kellie and took him prisoner. He was executed in Edinburgh.

Once Charles II was safely on the throne, the estates were handed back, and in 1682 the third Baronet, Lord High Chancellor of Scotland, was created first Earl of Aberdeen. His son, William, a Jacobite sympathiser, did not pay for his sympathies with his life, unlike his great uncle. Married for the third time, each wife grander than the one before, the ambitious Earl turned his attentions to acquiring yet more lands and money. His ambitions paid off. On the site of the ruined House of Kellie, allegedly using some of its original stones, William Adam, father of the renowned Adam brothers, was enlisted to build a mansion. Haddo House was more or less completed in 1732.

Where the old roads once ran like fault lines, a network of castles stretches across Aberdeenshire; family strongholds pinpointing those parts most vulnerable to attack. Out of a landscape scarred by its history, they are reminders of those troubled times: ruins of past fortifications, towers like sentries, still standing guard over the glens.

Haddo is quite different from these, its ancient neighbours. Nor does it show any of the later fashion for "Scottish baronial", fussily turreted and awkward. Though in fact it is Palladian in style, there is something rather English about Haddo, something quietly balanced and pleasing, set out on its smooth lawns. The centre block reaches the wings by gracefully curving covered corridors on either side. From the bottom of the Victoria avenue it has a sort of doll's house regularity of doors and windows. Perhaps the granite sets it apart. Bleached silver white in the early morning sun, it shines like washed grains of sand, shifting to the dusty gold of summer. By evening, as the light catches the house front on, the stone is stained rosy-pink.

The real stuff of an historic house is probably its paintings. Somehow they bring life to the past and substance to all the stories. In the big dining room, a neat-featured gentleman in a white powdered wig turns out to be "the wicked Earl". This rogue, the third Earl, neglected Haddo, his wife and children for no fewer than three brown-eyed mistresses and a clutch of bastards. Two of the extra households were just down the road.

His rightful heir did not live long enough to inherit. He was killed, falling from his horse, frightened by the sudden clanking of a pail being filled at the well of neighbouring Gight Castle. This was a haunted place, associated with witches, ghosts and a whirlpool, at the bottom of which the devil is said to sit on treasures stolen by an earlier Gordon. Legend has it that a diver sent down into the Hagberry Pot to retrieve the chest, emerged a gibbering madman. Sent down again, having first been tortured, "Better to face the Devil than the Laird o' Gight", his remains floated to the surface of the water, a ghastly headless corpse.

Lord Haddo's death itself fulfilled one part of a sinister prophecy, pronounced centuries before by Thomas the Rhymer:

> "When the heron leaves the tree
> The Laird o' gight shall landless be
> At Gight three men a violent death shall dee
> And efter that the lands shall lie in lea."

The fourth Earl of Aberdeen was a politician, first Foreign Secretary under Peel, then Prime Minister in the subsequent coalition Government. Despite his busy life, he still found time to improve his estate, planting some of the fourteen million young trees himself. His wife and daughters stayed at Haddo where, sadly, they died lingering deaths from consumption, one after the other, spending their days in what is now the library, the windows sealed because it was thought the fresh air was harmful. In 1946 my mother discovered their tiny notebooks, scarcely larger than a matchbox, hidden in a safe. Their portrait hangs over the main staircase: three pretty girls whose cheeks are deceptively rosy. Their father's political career ended too with a bitter blow. His Cabinet, very much against his wishes, set themselves to declaring war on Russia. Split by troubles, the Government fell and in 1854 the Crimean War broke out. A few years later the fourth Earl was dead, some say of a broken heart.

In the drawing room is another tale to tell: the mysterious disappearance of the sixth Earl. He was a young man when he inherited Haddo. At the time he was working in Canada as a lumberjack. The responsibilities of running an estate added to his worries over what were undoubtedly fairly modest debts. But George took fright. He rushed back to Canada where, using the alias George Osborne, he signed on as a sailor. Seeking excitement and adventure, George was keen to try the more dangerous routes round the Cape and the Horn. At this point in the story he simply disappeared. Not for seven months did his family discover what had really happened. First mate on a journey from Boston to Australia and China, hitting a storm soon after leaving port, George was swept overboard and drowned. But it was not for a further two years, after much detective work to prove he died unmarried, with no heir to

Haddo House

inherit, that any other claim to the title could be made. In 1872, after another brother had accidentally shot himself in 1868, Johnny was at last able to declare himself the rightful seventh Earl.

Not everyone has been charmed by Haddo. "Why have you brought me to this horrible house?" Seeing her new home for the first time on a foully cold day, the young bride burst into tears. She had just come twenty miles from Aberdeen with her husband, Johnny, the seventh Earl of Aberdeen, in an open barouche and could not conceal her dismay. Unprotected from damp easterly winds and harsh gales, the land seemed sour and mossy, planted with dark conifers. And, in 1878, Haddo itself was draughty and cold, without gas or hot water. The wind shrieked through the shutters, moaning and groaning in the long corridors. Ishbel immediately set about redecorating.

Johnny was quite happy to leave the handling of their finances to her, just as he allowed others to run his estate. Yet he willingly lent or gave money away even though at times he did not have it to give. By nature gentle and mild, he was a man of simple tastes and faith who nevertheless supported wholeheartedly his more unorthodox, strong-willed and energetic wife.

Ishbel, a staunch admirer of the suffragettes, had advanced ideas. At Haddo she started a Sunday school and encouraged the farm servants and housemaids to attend night classes. Chapel was attended daily by all the household. Wherever she went, the bad housing, lack of education and proper medical care of the poor appalled her. Ishbel wanted it all changed. Letters and articles were written, she gave talks and addressed meetings. Her audience, spellbound, were soon persuaded. The problem, as always, was money.

A friend and supporter of Gladstone and Home Rule, the seventh Earl was appointed Viceroy of Ireland. Straightaway, Ishbel threw her energies into the problems there, TB and poverty being among the worst. In 1893, Johnny became Governor General of Canada. Ishbel once more threw herself into women's causes. She had been elected President of the International Council of Women, and now she set to work to start up the Victorian Order of Nurses. Then, in 1905, following a second term in Ireland, the seventh Earl was created first Marquis of Aberdeen. And yet, by most, they were soon known more affectionately as "We Twa", the name borrowed from

"We Twa" stirring the pudding

the title of the autobiography they wrote together.

Soon the lack of funds turned into a crisis. Coming home from one of their collecting missions in America, they soon discovered with wartime shortages and their own over-spending, that they could not afford to live at Haddo and so had to move temporarily to an hotel in Aberdeen. Large parts of the estate were sold to settle debts and in 1916 Haddo and its estate was handed over to George, their son.

After her husband's death, Ishbel went on reading her bible but, eccentric as ever, turned to spiritualism, going to mediums and seances to keep in touch. Her habit of sitting up all night writing often led to her nodding off at the numerous meetings she still attended. No one dared wake her. But others were quick to criticise. She was scorned, called a "crank, a revolutionary, strong minded and high-handed". There were rumours she ate with her servants and played hide-and-seek with the housemaids and footmen. For the rest, her generosity and kindness were praised. These words in a letter from Canada thanking "We Twa" are typical: "You are loved here not so much for the financial start which you gave . . . but because of what you have felt for all your fellow men."

Uncle Doddie

While Ishbel may have wanted to devote all she had to improving the lot of her fellow-beings, thankfully some of the money was squeezed off and spent on Haddo. In the sunny and light morning room, the spicier smells of logs and satinwood furniture mingle with those of roses and sweetpeas. The fireplace and the pretty plaster ceiling are part of her improvements. Her own watercolours hang amongst the pictures, the large cabinet against the wall was a present from Johnny.

George, second Marquess of Aberdeen, was the eldest son of "We Twa", and my father's uncle. Even now, long after his death in 1965, he is too much part of the family to be thought of as "history". To everyone who came to Haddo he was known simply as "Uncle Doddy". In their position it would have been natural if "We Twa" had been a little disappointed at the woman their son and heir chose to marry. In fact there was only relief when, at the age of twenty-seven, Doddie married the widowed mother of his best friend at Oxford, a lady one year younger than his own mother. For Uncle Doddie suffered from epilepsy and there were fears he might pass on this affliction to succeeding generations. The marriage was not only a blessing for his family. For thirty years Doddie and Flo were perfectly happy. By all accounts his second marriage, to a childhood contemporary, was a disaster. Until she died, nine years later in 1949, they virtually lived apart.

In 1945, just after the war, Haddo was handed over, not to Doddie's brother, Dudley, but directly to his nephew, David Gordon, my father, who remained Laird of Haddo until his death in 1974.

Uncle Doddie remained very much in evidence there, coming out every weekend with Margaret Christie. Originally she had been his secretary but, as the years passed and he became older and somewhat more eccentric and absentminded, she cared for him as for a favourite child. In his turn, Uncle Doddie was devoted to her.

Perhaps living with him for so long had made Margaret slightly dotty too. Highly imaginative and wildly eccentric, to us she was the sort of person who never quite stopped being a child. Her name, after an obscure little rhyme thought up by my youngest brother, Jamie, was shortened from Maggie to Faggie and eventually to plain Fag, and may have had something to do with an uncharacteristic, almost naughty habit of smoking in the garden, while she was on her hands and knees weeding. She said it was to keep the midgies away.

Uncle Doddie, Marquis of Aberdeen, holding the baby.

We visited them in their house outside Aberdeen on Fridays, running through the open door to cries of "Coo-ee, coo-ee!". Seeing Fag jump up to hug us all, Uncle Doddie would put down *The Press and Journal* and give a huge shout of delight. He could never remember us from one weekend to the other but was always immensely pleased to see us.

Below the drawing room was an old summerhouse, open at the

front. We lay back on the faded cushions of the wicker chairs while, puffing and blowing, Fag pushed and the summerhouse, revolving on its axle, sailed slowly round like an ancient creaking roundabout. Or we played the "magic piano", the pianola, as Uncle Doddie whirled unsteadily about the room. Jamie could not yet reach the pedals so one of us, lying on our stomachs at his feet, had to pump the pedals by hand.

Afterwards, we were all driven out to Haddo. Still like a child unable to part with its favourite toy, Fag took her treasured possessions with her. Inside her battered brown suitcase, as world-travelled as she, were her poetry books, the postcards of all the places she had been to: Iceland, Spain, India, the Holy Land; the curious bits and pieces collected from her beloved islands: Fetlar, Soay, St Kilda; feathers she had picked up on her walks, bits of driftwood, stones and shells; bead necklaces and brooches and, most important of all, Pushkin, a small gray stuffed mouse with real teeth and fur.

One day Fag astonished everyone who was sitting quietly through in the morning room by rushing in in her petticoat, clutching yards and yards of brilliantly dyed material. One end wrapped round her, she made someone else stand at the far side of the room with the other end. Not waiting to explain herself, she began to spin round and round across the floor, winding and wrapping it about her like a cocoon. Only then did it become clear she had been having difficulty dressing herself in her new sari.

Uncle Doddie's increasing vagueness was an endearing if at times embarrassing quality. Even those who loved him best could not deny that the day had finally come for him to retire from his duties as Lord Lieutenant of Aberdeenshire. One summer, in that odd green shieling from which the Royal Family watch the annual Braemar Gathering, he graciously introduced the Queen to the Queen Mother!

From the side, round by the back door, the way used by everyday folk, Haddo is a sprawling mass of pinkish gray granite, dissected by windows and broken angles of roof. The clock sits high on the wall over the arch leading to the courtyard, its round sky-blue face below the helter-skelter weathercock tower.

Just before the courtyard, to the right, is the garden gate, one of eight, all kept carefully closed because of the rabbits. Inside, four acres are laid out on several different levels. Gravel paths lead across the flat square of the upper terrace, past stone urns and marble seats. Around the curved stone basin of the fountain, set in the centre of the lawn, are rose beds, formally arranged in symmetrical patterns, edged with ridges of stone, sunken and moss-furred. On three sides the terrace slopes down to the herbaceous borders and the more informal garden of our childhood: the long grass and the lime avenue whose trees are so old they lean towards one another as though for support, gray branches arching to meet like the ribcage of a great skeleton.

To me, when I was a child, Haddo seemed more like a town. Essentially, the south wing, reached through the courtyard, was the family wing, but the arrangement was very elastic. All those years the four of us were growing up, people came and went, an overflow that often spilled into the rest of the house. Sometimes it was difficult not to mind when the interest in us became an intrusion. Once, fed up with it all, Sarah banged loudly on her bedroom window, shouting "Go away!" to a car-load of sightseers who had driven through the policies and were wandering over the front lawn taking photographs. They rushed back to their car, quite startled.

For me anyway, amongst the most fascinating of those who came to Haddo were all the different ageing aunts:

> Old Aunt Adela came to tea
> When I was nine.
> Sitting in the distance
> At the end of the Big Dining Room table.
> Ignoring her sister,
> Great Aunt Ida,
> Cracked skin and a cracked voice.
> Very grand.
> They wore jewels for breakfast.
> Necklaces outshining the chandeliers,
> Huge purple plums of glass,
> On their ugly Drummond hands.
> Noses you could hang a teacup on.
> We had to be very careful.
>
> Through in the Premier's end,
> Aunt Winnie, waiting;

Aunt May and Deedie long since dead.
Every afternoon we had to be nice, remembering,
Aunt Deedie, crippled, in a prefab, on the Isle of Wight.
Aunt May at the top of a long dim stair.
(There were white currants in a china bowl)
All three, skinny as birds, in hats.
Aunt Winnie smoked; too much, too late.
Gasping, her lizard's mouth dried up with scarlet.
Backs straight, we played Old Maid,
and she didn't seem to mind.
Still we were careful.
Uncle Doddie, in his kilt, chose the wrong chair,
Fell off, roaring with laughter, backwards.
When Winnie was in bed, dying,
A man with red hair came and stood smiling.
Great Uncle Archie's ghost.

Great Aunt Marjorie outlived them all,
Leaving for a little while,
Poor Cousin Peggy,
Silent and anorexic,
A gray shadow of Mother.
Aunt Marjorie, nearly ninety,
Went to Cuba,
In fawn socks, neatly folding her ankles.
Washing her hair with egg yolk.
Gaunt figures in a museum house of photographs,
Colder than a chapel,
Keeping string and scraps of wrapping paper,
Frugally saving it all for History.

The twenty-two bedrooms, almost all of which can sleep at least two people, give some idea of the size of a Haddo house-party. As children, because of the comings and goings, we learned how to make ourselves invisible. There was our own bit of garden. We climbed all over the rockery, moving the stones about, looking for worms and creepy-crawlies and our lost tortoise who lived there from time to time with a companionable toad. We even had our own Wendy House, though being placed immediately below the nursery it was scarcely the ideal place to withdraw for a bit of peace and quiet, even with the door firmly closed and curtains drawn.

Down by the trees and bushes at the bottom of the garden, a hummock of land rose like an island, screened by beeches and a rambling untidy rhododendron bush whose brittle branches had shattered, leaving a natural maze of tunnels and low rooms; the perfect hideaway. We called it "The Labratry". The beeches were built like sailing ships. We were good climbers. Far above the ground, hidden in the rigging of their branches, we roosted like birds, keeping a lookout. The estate itself was our proper territory: we knew almost every inch of it. With all that vast space available to disappear into, we had a freedom others could scarcely imagine.

Past the morning room, a long red stair goes up to the bedrooms in the Square — the second floor in the centre block of the house. Above is another floor still, the attics, a dim dusty place with a central passageway off which are the tiny boxrooms slept in by the housemaids in "We Twa's" day. The wallpaper is brownish, stained with damp; hardly any light comes from the narrow skylights in the sloping roof. Each room had its own fireplace and a grate just big enough to burn a handful of sticks.

Other stairs go all the way from the Big Kitchen, up the three floors to the attics. Though there is a door at either end and doors at each intervening landing, going there was a test of bravey. Narrow and windowless, the stairs continue up between the walls: a staircase in a cupboard, claustrophobic, terrifying. Irresistible, in other words. Like mice, we scampered up and down, going secretly from one floor to another.

Sometimes, playing in the forbidden Square, we heard noises coming from the attics: slow footsteps, something heavy being dragged across the floor, a distant banging from the furthest boxroom. Sometimes there were real footsteps coming up the red stair and we had to dive under the fourposter beds or between the sheets, wriggling down next to the long sausage-shaped bolsters.

In the years after the war, large parties of friends and relations came to stay in the summer; a chance for them to go fishing and shooting, to play tennis, doze on the lawn, eat too much and generally enjoy themselves. Out on the terrace babies were lined up in old-fashioned prams. There were afternoon walks with nannies and dogs. Some of the visiting nannies were dreadfully haughty and grand, all the way from the south and quite a lot of feuding went on in the nursery. The grown-ups visited us from time to time as

Prams at Haddo, author in second from left

though we were in a sort of quarantine, sticking their noses round the door before quickly going away again.

Along at their end of the house, things were not always much better for all the aunts and uncles who, after several weeks of over-indulgence, were feeling liverish and out-of-sorts, fed up with the weather and a little bored with their own company. When it became too much like being cooped up on an ocean-going liner, my mother, with ghastly enthusiasm, would organise a picnic. It was compulsory.

We would go to the sea, straggling like refugees over the sands, carrying rugs and towels and spades, gallon thermoses of soup and great biscuit tins of sandwiches, enough for forty. Crouched in the dunes, out of the wind, the grown-ups were snappish, grumbling as if it were all some kind of punishment; lying muffled from head to foot in tartan rugs, laid out like so many mummies for burial.

If there was a quiet time at Haddo it was when winter storms cut us off from the outside world and we watched from the nursery window a raging whiteness that soon filled up the little roads in and out of the policies. Gales and blizzards frequently brought down the power lines, leaving us with neither telephone nor electricity. Then the Tilley lamps were fetched from the "Black Hole" under the stairs and filled with paraffin, the wicks and mantles carefully renewed. We did our homework distracted by shadows thrown up by the flickering oily-yellow light and listened to the battering of the wind outside, glad not to have to go to school in the gamekeeper's van which smelled strongly of rabbit.

Every morning the gray tractor came down from the gardens, towing the wooden snow plough, weighted down by sandbags and men, sitting silent , buried under folds of sacking. In the woods our own homemade ploughs left furrows and small tracks in the snow, criss-crossing one another as we went on an inspection of our secret hideouts. Sarah knitted nose protectors from odd bits of wool; held on by loops which went over our ears, they were the size of thistles.

As the years went by things were changing. The Haddo House Choral and Operatic Society had been in existence since 1946, founded by our parents. Now it was growing faster and faster. Since my father took over Haddo there had been carols in the chapel at Christmas time. Soon there was an opera at Easter. At first it was usually Gilbert and Sullivan, something fairly lighthearted and well known, then there was Verdi, Bizet, Puccini's *Turandot*, Vaughan-Williams's rarely performed *The Poisoned Kiss*.

No sooner had the orchestra packed thier violins and oboes than it was time to come back for the May concert. Again there was a lull before rehearsals began for the play and those who came up to spend their holidays at Haddo were the cast. The mood of the house changed to fit the production. Days were spent rehearsing and painting scenery. Bits of furniture began to disappear from the house down to the Hall. This large wooden building, green then, black now, with its high sloping shingled roof is the home of the Choral. After their years in Canada, "We Twa" decided to build the community centre they started at Haddo in the style of a Canadian village hall. There was a time when the list of past productions, mostly Shakespeare, was printed on the back of the Choral programme. Now there is not enough room for them all!

Haddo is usually a relaxed, if not relaxing, fairly informal sort of place. May concerts are somewhat different. At such moments we were aware of a certain tension; more poeple than ever rushing about, getting lost in the corridors, making sandwiches in the kitchen. All that kind of thing goes on, just as before: cellos parked against the furniture, queues at mealtimes, every single bedroom is full. Whether all the excitement is to do with the grandeur and importance of the music or the grandeur and importance of the musicians is hard to tell. The soloists are often famous names. Some of the orchestras have been coming to play at Haddo for years. As a small child I can recall hearing shrieks from the Square, soaring higher and higher, as the leading soprano ran through her scales in the Queen's bedroom. And from the woods floated sounds of a trumpet being played.

I remember four of us sitting on the wall above the rockery in the first spring sunshine to listen. Sounds spilled out through the wooden walls of the hall as though from a musical box. Later on, when I was old enough to be part of the proper audience, it made much more sense. This was the real purpose of our mother's life. Splendidly dressed, tall and remote on the rostrum, arms outstretched, she stood to conduct and we looked at her with new eyes. Yet to hear the birds singing in the trees outside, bursting their throats with enthusiastic rivalry, or a tractor going past, was reassuring. We knew as we played on the terrace not to shout or make a noise; the courtyard clock was stopped and, as a precaution, the poor dogs had to be shut inside. The concerts were a success, a triumph, so much so that on one occasion nobody noticed the soprano being sick into the flower arrangement at her feet.

In many ways Haddo is still a community centre, an organisation even. Its nerve-ends reach ever further afield drawing people from far outside its original area to come and take part. They arrive off planes and trains. Sadly there is no longer the unmistakable bulk of our father sitting at the back with the basses but there are Gordon faces in the choir: Aunt Jessamine and her brother, Alistair, now the sixth Marquess of Aberdeen; one coming from Wick, the other from Berkshire to meet at Haddo and continue the tradition. My mother conducts under the name of June Gordon.

We were the last children to be brought up in Haddo House. In 1979 the house was handed over to the National Trust for Scotland. In the south wing nothing much has changed. Our mother still rules the roost. Like the ever-changing cast of a play, people still come and go. The Choral is coming up for middle age but shows no sign of slowing down. Quite the opposite. Occasionally, my mother, waist-deep in the herbaceous border, is accused by a tourist of stealing the flowers. She does all the arrangements for the house just as she always has, even those rooms open to the public.

Quite simply, what is missing from Haddo is David, our father. An enormous man, almost always in a kilt, wearing the special socks knitted by our mother. The kilt gave the impression of being very old, not shabby exactly but certainly faded, even threadbare in places as though nibbled by generations of moths. A sporran rested comfortably on his large stomach. Made from an otter's head, its polished nose and button-bright eyes gave the sporran more the look of a benign, well-worn and much-loved teddy bear.

Like Uncle Doddie before him my father was so well known and distinctive that he stood out. In Aberdeen in a crowd of shoppers he could have been spotted half a mile away. Even when we were children, in a room of people, we could always tell where he was. Somehow, by comparison, everyone else seemed rather small. It was more than just his physical size.

One summer we stayed a few days in the Isle of Wight. The first evening, as darkness was falling, leaving my mother knitting the socks, he took us for a walk. There was just Sarah and myself: the boys were still at school. We ended up in a quiet road of small houses, set back from the street lamps. Keeping to the shadows we crept into gardens, along paths, peering through windows into the rooms of strangers. Perhaps he wanted to spy on the ordinary folk sitting inside, a kind of retaliation for all those afternoon visitors who could come and look round his home. To us who had never known him like this before he was, endearingly, like a naughty small boy.

How would we have explained it if he had been caught, if someone had looked up and caught the fourth Marquess of Aberdeen staring at them in their sitting room? Most likely, he would have charmed them with an invitation to stay at Haddo, for the whole summer if they wished, to sing or act, to bring their children, or elderly aunt or dog, their fishing rod and gun. They would have joined the production that is Haddo, confused at first, then happy.

The trouble is, having once been, they would have
had to come back. Everybody does.
That is the thing about Haddo.

Auld Wat

Jean Polwarth

HARDEN

Harden stands high above a glen of oak trees on a rocky bluff like a sentinel guarding the Scottish border. In this year of grace, 1986, it is a comfortable home, ready to accommodate the needs of a large family as they come and go. No "stately home", but, with its kitchen and nurseries, its log fires, and its well-stocked vegetable garden, it will always be at the heart of the family. But Harden was not always so peaceful a home: its story has reflected the clash and claver of Scottish history as closely as it has recorded the ups and downs of the Scott family who lived there.

On moonlit nights it is easy to imagine the moss-troopers awaiting the signal to mount their ponies for yet another raid into Liddesdale. It was these raids across the border which provided their livelihood in the shape of English cattle, on which their wives and children could feast. Their leader, the bearded Auld Wat of Harden, was loyal and fearless as he guided his men across the bogs and peathags of the Debateable Lands — so called because the Scots and the English could never quite decide where their boundaries lay in this wild country of rounded hills and rushing burns. A full moon was vital for these raids, and so the moon has always been important to the Scotts of Harden. It is depicted in their coat of arms, and it lights the border hills with its silvery rays more often than the fleeting sunshine of a Scottish summer. With no moon, raiding would have been impossible. The Scott family motto is "Reparabit Cornua Phoebe" — "There will be moonlight again". Today, the youngest Scott of Harden bears the name Phoebe — she is three years old.

Life at Harden in the sixteenth century must have been uncomfortable, crowded into small draughty rooms with a strong aroma of cow-dung carried from the ground floor when the beasts

Harden

"in-wintered". The first Harden was a Peel Tower, standing stark and grim above Harden Glen, looking out towards distant Carter Bar and the big Cheviot. It was essentially an outpost from which

Auld Wat Scott and his men could set out to provide their winter stores — cattle from the English pastures in Cumberland and Northumberland; stores which could be neatly herded into the glen or "beeftub" below the tower at Harden, a convenient larder for the Scott family's needs. When this larder was empty, Wat's fair wife Mary Scott — the Flower of Yarrow — would indicate the fact by serving her lord and master with a pair of gilt spurs on a platter, as a gentle hint. This was the signal for Wat of Harden to set out on an excursion across the border with his trusty men.

Wat Scott had succeeded his father, William Scott, as Laird of Harden in 1563, and on his marriage to Mary Scott of Dryhope he acquired another Peel Tower in the valley of Yarrow. His family already owned the tower of Kirkhope in Ettrick valley, so now he had three towers, strategically placed from east to west, in Borthwick-water, Ettrick and Yarrow. These three towers were situated in a direct line between Yarrow and Teviotdale, as the crow flies — or as the moss-troopers galloped on moonlit nights. Wat's marriage, unlike many that were entered into purely for additional power and lands, proved to be a happy one, and the couple rejoiced in four sons and six daughters.

The family knew they were safe at Harden, for the situation of the fortress was one of the best in the Borders, immeasurably superior to Buccleuch's own Peel Tower at Branxholm; possibly even more so than Hermitage Castle, the great fortification built on the very border in the thirteenth century by Walter Comyn, Earl of Menteith, who had been appointed by the King of Scotland to strengthen the Scottish defences against the English.

But Auld Wat was not one to stay cowering in his Peel Tower, and he soon gained a reputation as the greatest reiver, or free-booter, in the Borders. His raids were like a game of chess, as he moved his steel-bonneted men from fortress to fortress until they faced the border itself. They were courageous men, and Auld Wat had great pride in his moss-troopers as they rode their stocky horses surefooted over bog and crag, with the moon glinting on the steel of their helmets, ready at all times to clash with the English.

There were strange rules for this game of beggar-my-neighbour; the "hot-trod" was one of them. The hot-trod was devised to give a victim a sporting chance in the final pursuit, for when first captured he was let loose again, and given a few minutes start before his pursuers galloped after him once more. But this was no game of cat and mouse: the men who lived on either side of the border, whether Scots or English, were equally matched in strength and cunning. They undoubtedly had a secret admiration for each other, just as today they have so much in common. The feeling of kinship, coupled with friendly rivalry, has remained strong, and both Scots and English on either side of the border still bear the great local names of Scott, Graham, Elliot, Kerr, Douglas, Hume, Turnbull and Armstrong.

Auld Wat was adept at foraging for his needs across the border. "If yon haystack had legs, I would drive it hame," he is supposed to have joked. But one day his foraging caused an unexpected repercussion for his wife and family. He had set out from Harden to raid the lands of Rede, which belonged to the Neville family. The opposition was stronger than Auld Wat had expected, and Neville himself was killed in the fray, and his castle burnt to the ground. In making their escape, driving their stolen cattle, Auld Wat and his men had to cross the height of the land at Carter Bar. Once they were safely across the border, Auld Wat allowed them a breather, for

"The Haugh is ringing wi' Harden's men."

it had been a fast chase up the steep pass. It was a fine spring day, the sun shone, the cuckoos called, the bunch of stolen cattle lowed, and a soft breeze blew to cool the panting moss-troopers and to still the heaving flanks of their tired ponies. But Auld Wat felt sad; it grieved him to cause bloodshed. He even imagined he could see wisps of smoke drifting over the hill from the burning homestead of the Neville family. As he cupped his hands in a burn to drink deeply, he heard a cry above the gurgling of the water. He raised his head and listened again; it sounded like a distant whaup. Then he heard it once more, nearer and louder. Suddenly he knew that this was no whaup, it was the cry of a newborn child. Auld Wat turned on his men. Who had done this dastardly deed? To burn an Englishman's castle and to put him to the sword was not shameful in itself, but to steal a defenceless child was utterly dishonourable.

Auld Wat made his men open their knapsacks, one by one, until he found what he was looking for — wrapped in a shawl, concealed by the man's homespun plaid, lay a fair-haired baby boy. This man would hang from the great Hanging Tree at Harden on their return

"Saw the horses as they faced the glen,
And the shadows gather the Harden men."

home, Auld Wat roared. Meanwhile there was nothing to be done by an honourable man but to take the Neville child home to his wife and bring him up as one of his own family.

And so the Neville boy was reared by the Flower of Yarrow, and he was nicknamed "The Whaup" by her other children. How different he looked to the black-haired Scott brothers and sisters with their brown eyes. How English he was, with his fair hair and blue eyes, and his love of books and music. But they loved him as a brother, and Auld Wat and his wife Mary counted him as their own child. When he reached manhood, however, he did not have the same desire to feud and fight like the Scott boys. He seemed to guess that his birthright lay elsewhere, though no one had told him. For one day he took a pony and rode across the border, like a homing pigeon, until he reached the Rede.

His widowed mother had kept the family lands together, and rebuilt the castle. She knew it was her long-lost son as soon as she saw him riding over the hill. Great was their joy at being reunited, and his mother told young Neville that she had never doubted that he would find his own lands again one day.

Back at Harden, Auld Wat guessed the truth of young Neville's disappearance, and smiled to himself with satisfaction. He had repaid his debt of honour.

Probably the most famous story of Auld Wat was the part he played in the celebrated rescue of Kinmont Willie from Carlisle Castle in 1596. It is one of the most thrilling incidents in Borders history. Kinmont Willie was an Armstrong, and he shared Auld Wat's fame as one of the bravest Borderers of the times; a man of great ability, with outstanding physical and moral qualities, and with considerable military genius.

It was on a day in March that Kinmont Willie was attacked by a body of two hundred English Borderers as he returned home, on a "day of truce" (between the Scots and the English), along the banks of the Liddle. The English were led by Salkeld, the deputy of Lord Scrope, Lord Warden, who was the warden of the East March. This was one of the areas in which Kinmont Willie's raids had taken place, although the West and Middle Marches had suffered even more at his hands.

Kinmont Willie was chased for some miles, captured, tied to the body of his horse and thus carried in triumph by the English to

Auld Wat of Harden, *Tom Scott, ARSA.*

Carlisle Castle. As he had been attending a warden court to discuss a territorial dispute, Salkeld's act was in direct violation of border law, which guaranteed freedom from molestation to all who might be present at the warden court on a day of truce, between sunrise on one day and sunrise on the next.

Scrope was to excuse this manifest breach in border law by saying that Willie Armstrong was taken beyond the limits of his charge, and that he had broken the assurance taken at the warden court. Both charges were undoubtedly false, for Kinmont Willie would never have gone to the warden court if he had not felt sure that he was amply protected from arrest by these ancient laws. The fact that he and his friends had been guilty of many outrages on the English border, and that the Lord Warden, Scrope, was justified in regarding him as a "rank reiver", were not relevant to the specific case.

Nevertheless, the English government seemed determined to detain Kinmont Willie until such time as they could conveniently put an end to his reiving by hanging him on Haribee Hill. But they had forgotten that Kinmont Willie's greatest ally was "the Bold Buccleuch" himself. The account of Willie's capture was speedily conveyed to Branxholm, and the news was accepted with great indignation, as the balladist tells us:

> "He [Buccleuch] has ta'en the table wi' his hand,
> He garr'd the red wine spring on hie —
> Now Christ's curse on my head, he said,
> But avenged on Lord Scroope I'll be!"

Buccleuch's first act was to send a messenger the few miles from Branxholm to Harden to tell his kinsman, Auld Wat, that they had important business to do in Carlisle. If he was to free Kinmont Willie from Carlisle Castle, the one man he needed at his side was Auld Wat, whose white beard belied his vigour and his cunning.

On a dark tempestuous night, Buccleuch and Harden met two hundred of their bravest followers at the tower of Morton, a fortalice in the Debateable Lands, on the water of Sark, some ten miles or so from Carlisle. The plans had been laid the previous day at a horse-race at Langholm. The rain had been falling heavily, and the Esk and the Eden were in raging flood. Auld Wat's men carried with them scaling ladders and crowbars, hand-picks and axes, and were prepared to take the castle by storm.

The first task of the night was to dispose of Scrope's deputy, Salkeld. This was speedily accomplished with a lance by Dickie of Dryhope: "Then nevir a word had Dickie to say, Sae he thrust the lance through his fause bodie."

Now the way was clear for the advance upon the castle. It was the darkest night any of them had ever seen, and for once Auld Wat was glad there was no moon. The rain came down in torrents and the thunder rolled. "But t'was wind and weet, and fire and sleet, when we came beneath the castle wa'."

But now there was a serious setback: the ladders were too short; finding a postern, however, they undermined it and soon made a breach big enough for a soldier to pass through. Buccleuch and Auld Wat managed to squeeze through and were able to disarm and bind the watch. Then they opened the postern from the inside to admit their companions. Twenty-four of their men rushed to the castle jail while Buccleuch kept the postern. Auld Wat led the men to the jail, forcing the door of the chamber where Kinmont Willie was confined, and soon had him out, still in his irons. He sounded a trumpet — the signal he and Buccleuch had agreed on — to be answered in return by Buccleuch's own trumpet, at which point their men swarmed into the base court of the castle.

By now Scrope's men had sounded their own alarm, to be answered by the cathedral bell and the town house bell. A beacon was lit on the top of the great tower, which increased the panic of the English — for the red glare of the fire on the blackness of the night, and on the shadowy steel-clad forms of the Borderers, made it impossible to tell whether the castle had been attacked by a hundred men or a thousand. The confusion and dismay was increased by the suddenness of the attack, and by the terrific noise made by Buccleuch's men as they laid siege to the castle. Lord Scrope decided that discretion was the better part of valour, and kept close within his chamber. Nothing was seen or heard of the Lord Warden that night.

As Kinmont Willie was borne aloft on the shoulders of one of Auld Wat's strongest men, Red Rowan, "the starkest man in Teviotdale", he shouted a lusty "good night" to the bewildered Lord Warden:

"Farewell, farewell, my gude Lord Scroope!
My gude Lord Scroope, farewell!" he cried,
"I'll pay you for my lodging maill,
When first we meet on the border side."

Buccleuch now joined Auld Wat, having accomplished their purpose, and their men left the castle to find their horses, which they quickly mounted. Now they had to cross a raging torrent before they were safely back in Scotland. The Eden Water was swollen to twice its normal size with the rainstorm, and was still rising. But, "even where it flowed frae bank to brim", they plunged their horses into the swirling waters, and "safely swam the stream". Buccleuch and Auld Wat stood shoulder to shoulder with Kinmont Willie as they all three looked at the glow of Carlisle Castle in the darkness. While Kinmont Willie cocked a snook at his erstwhile captors, the Bold Buccleuch called across the raging torrent:

"If ye like na my visit in merry England,
In fair Scotland come visit me."

Auld Wat of Harden's shaggy white hair and beard streamed out in the wind as he took his last look at the castle they had stormed. Then he turned to his friend, Willie Armstrong, to suggest that they now make their way to a local smith he knew, whose cottage lay on the roadside between Longtown and Langholm. Kinmont Willie looked ruefully at the irons which still bound his legs, then burst into a throaty laugh:

"O mony a time, quo' Kinmont Willie,
I've pricked a horse out oure the furs;
But since the day I back'd a steed,
I never wore sic cumbrous spurs!"

The smith had soon knocked the irons off his legs, and the three men returned triumphantly to Teviotdale on horseback. Little did Kinmont Willie, Bold Buccleuch and Auld Wat of Harden know that men were already declaring that there had been nothing like the rescue of Kinmont Willie from Carlisle Castle since the days of Sir William Wallace.

When King James VI of Scotland ascended the English throne, he issued a decree that all raids between England and Scotland must cease. This meant that if Auld Wat was to keep his beeftub filled he must raid his Scots neighbours instead. From ancient documents it is known that his neighbours, Walter Scott of Coldielands and Gideon Murray of Elibank, were forced to petition the King for authority to "demolish the houses and fortalices of Harden, and Dryhope, belonging to Walter Scott of Harden". Auld Wat was to see his own Peel Tower burnt down on numerous occasion as his victims took their revenge on him. But he continued to live at Harden, patiently rebuilding his tower each time they "dinged it doon".

Auld Wat was now in his sixties and beginning to tire of his raiding activities, especially if it meant stealing from his kinsmen. His son William, on the other hand, entered eagerly into the forays, until he was careless enough to be caught red-handed by Sir Gideon Murray of Elibank, in 1611.

William Scott was kept a prisoner in Elibank Castle, on the banks of the Tweed, close to the doom-tree on which he was to hang for his folly. Each day he was brought his gruel by one of his captor's three daughters. The youngest was a plain girl with freckles and an unusually large mouth. Her name was Agnes.

William laughingly called her "Meg with the muckle mouth" and amused himself by complimenting her on her looks. Her mother heard his remarks and saw that her daughter liked them. She suggested to her husband, Sir Gideon, that their captive was handsome, as the Scotts of Harden tended to be; that he was heir to a fine estate and unmarried. Why not wed poor ugly Agnes to him, instead of hanging him? Sir Gideon thought it over for a while and then agreed. It was not such a bad idea after all.

But he had not taken into account young William Scott's pride, or the courage he had inherited from his father, Auld Wat of Harden.

> "Lead on to the gallows, then Willie replied,
> I'm now in your power and ye carry it high.
> Nae daughter of yours shall e'er lie by my side;
> A Scott, ye mon mind, counts it naethin' to die."

But after this first outburst, William Scott of Harden reflected that life was good in this bonny border country, so he consented to Sir Gideon's suggestion and the marriage contract was drawn up straightaway, written on the parchment of the drum which was about to be beaten to announce the hanging, according to Sir Walter Scott, whose pen brought all the old Borders ballads and legends so vividly alive once more. Willie Scott of Harden had married the plainest of the three Murray daughters, but at least he had kept his life.

The marriage contract is still kept safely at Harden, protected by its original calfskin outer covering. The bridegroom's father, Auld Wat, had to append his signature, which he did with a cross, being unable to write. To Auld Wat of Harden there was no doubt in his mind that the sword would always be mightier than the pen.

William's marriage turned out, against all odds, to be a happy one. In their old age Auld Wat and his wife Mary were able to enjoy nine grandchildren from this union. In addition, Agnes Murray had brought as her tocher another Peel Tower, the fortress of Oakwood near Selkirk. The Scotts of Harden were now amongst the greatest landowners in the Borders and it was from one of these grandsons, Walter — known as Wat Wadspurs, to distinguish him from his grandfather, Auld Wat — that Sir Walter Scott of literary fame descended. Auld Wat lived to the ripe age of eighty-four. His son and heir died in 1655, at an advanced age like his father before him.

The moon still shines on the old house, now no longer a Peel Tower but a comfortable family house with low-ceilinged rooms, designed by a later William Scott of Harden, who was made Earl of Tarras (for his life only) when he married the little Buccleuch heiress, Mary, as his child-bride. Sadly she died, and her younger sister inherited the Buccleuch title and married the Duke of Monmouth. Tarras married again, this time to the heiress Helen Hepburne of Humbie, and once more there were dark-haired, brown-eyed Scott children playing in the beeftub under the oak trees. There will always be Scotts at Harden, still a sentinel on its high rock, with the moon inspiring its lairds to greater things.

Reparabit Cornua Phoebe.

The Ghost Stays Put

Alan Bell Macdonald

RAMMERSCALES

It was a bitterly cold day in January 1764 in Lochmaben cemetery as the mortal remains of Dr James Mounsey of Rammerscales were being laid to rest. There were very few mourners and they stood huddled in a group on one side of the grave while the coffin was slowly lowered into its depths. On the other side stood a tall man wrapped in a long black cloak with a fur hat pulled well down over his face. Motionless he looked down at the grave. As the coffin descended he caught sight of the name on the plate and smiled sardonically. It was his own! It was not often, he thought, that after attending one's own funeral one could return to one's house and sink into anonymity.

He walked slowly down the lane from the cemetery to the wide road that cut through the little village, deserted now under a leaden sky. The fine snow was being whipped along, driven by a relentless east wind. The small thatched cottages crouched under the lash of the tempest. He shivered, drawing his heavy cloak more tightly round him and pulled his fur hat even further over his eyes. Only his coach, slowly whitening in the gathering snowstorm, broke the empty space of the roadway. He turned down the street a few paces and knocked heavily on the door of the drinking shop where he knew his coachman would be. The blows from his leaded stick were answered at once, the door opened and he stepped into the room. There were quite a lot of people there and most of them knew who he was, or thought they did.

"We're sorry about your brother, a fine mon, we coulda done wi' mair like him in the district — will ye no hae a dram wi' us, it's starvation outside."

The conversation picked up again as he accepted a glass of whisky, bowing to the assembled company and thanking them for their sympathy. He had been away in Russia so long there was no danger of his being recognised — even his coachman was unaware of the deception. The raw spirit coursed through him and in the warmth of the room his blood began to circulate again. He spoke a few words to those nearest him and, gesturing to his coachman, he bade the company goodbye and went out again into the snow. It was not unlike Russia, he thought, looking across the street at the long line of low houses stretching away into the white distance. He climbed into the coach and mantled himself in the huge bearskin rug while they set off slowly on the three-mile journey to the house.

"What a homecoming," he thought despondently. All his high hopes were dashed. He had achieved the highest positions in Russian medical circles: Archiater and Chief Director of the Medical Chancery and of the whole Medical Faculty throughout the Russian Empire, with the rank of Privy Councillor. He rolled the majestic titles off his tongue with a rueful smile — and he hadn't had

Rammerscales in the snow, *Scottish Field*

to commit murder to achieve them! But murder had ensured that he would never enjoy them again. How ironical! Once Czar Peter had been assassinated he knew the writing was on the wall for him. Ever since the death of the Empress Elizabeth on Christmas day 1761 many eyes had turned in his direction. He knew that Czar Peter was very unpopular for his pro-Prussion bias and he had realised full well that the Ukase affirming him in those positions of state would be a death sentence if Peter were assassinated. Within six months of his accession he had been murdered, and his wife Catherine, no doubt privy to the bloody affair, became his successor. He had felt threatened under the new regime and lost no time in tendering his resignation to the Czarina on the grounds of ill-health. His discharge had been signed on August 20th, 1762, and he left the country, travelling fast across Europe to Paris and so home, leaving his effects to follow by sea. His wife had already left the country and was staying with one of his three daughters who were married and lived in the south of England. His three sons too were now well established.

The coach lurched along the road beside the loch, the low silhouette of Lochmaben Castle barely visible through the blown snow. He loved this Dumfriessshire countryside. Having been born sixty-four years ago at Skipmyre, not a dozen miles away, he had always had a yearning to return one day and build a house nearby. So he had bought Rammerscales Estate at the judicial sale of Robert Carruthers who had followed the fortunes of the Jacobites once too often and had thereby lost his own. In those days, when his life had been full of optimism, Dr Mounsey had commissioned the building of a fine square mansion house in lovely pale pink sandstone from the recently opened quarries at Corncockle. Now his beautiful house was finished, though scarcely ready for habitation. The disastrous happenings in Moscow had spoilt his plans and, apart from having to return earlier than planned, he was no longer a high-powered physician at the court of the Czarina, but a hunted man. He was fully aware that his vertiginous fall from grace in Moscow would probably not end here since he had had enemies. Nobody in his position among equally powerful groups surrounding the ruler with their Byzantine plots and counter-plots could hope not to be suspected of treachery. There had been an attempt on his life in Leith docks at the time his belongings were being unloaded after their journey from St Petersburg. This had surprised and alarmed him a good deal. The wound in his shoulder was still painful.

As a result of all this he had organised the involved charade of his own death and burial with the appropriate notices in the prints that would be likely to catch the eye of the Czarina's secret police and other groups that might wish him ill. Some people, apart from his family, had had to be let into the secret and indeed some of them laughed at his fears, saying that he was suffering from a persecution complex, and that he was carrying the whole affair to ludicrous lengths. They would certainly laugh now, he thought, as the coach turned off the main road and began the long climb to the mansion house, if they could see the alterations he had made to it after the attempt on his life. Virtually every room in the house now had two, if not three, exits and entrances, each one consisting of double doors with space between in the thickness of the wall where a person could wait listening and move out to one side or the other as the pursuers were following. He also had a secondary narrow stairway constructed from the top to the bottom of the house, and from the cellars he could slip out to hide in a walled-up cave, once an ice-house, now camouflaged by the hillside where he could lie hidden until the pursuit drew off. But there was always danger, they could be waiting for him now at the top of the hill; he had his carriage pistols, the lead-headed stick, and a short sword. He would give a good account of himself. He sighed and murmured again: "What a homecoming!"

As the coach slowly climbed the last few hundred yards the snow thickened though the wind had abated since the house was well sheltered by the hill behind and big plantations on either side. Dr Mounsey climbed out, thanked the old coachman and said he could make for the stables and retire for the night as he would not be needed again. Though still early in the afternoon, it was nearly dark. The snow still fell, stealthily, perpetually settling, filling the carriage tracks and masking the uneven ground to a level expanse of white. The doctor stood in the shelter of the porch half-fascinated by the snow swirling away into the distance. Finally he shook off his cloak, stamped his feet and entered the house. A faint light filtered under the door of the room on the right. He threw his cloak and fur hat on the settee in the hall, the two pillars standing ghostly in the half-light, and the fine spiral staircase rising in the distance to the next floor. He opened the door of the sitting room carefully with sacrcely a sound. He looked round and relaxed; he would surely have sensed it had there been anyone hiding in the shadows. The candles were lit and there was a big fire beside which he sat down and began thinking.

Arranging your own funeral and being officially dead could very well cause some problems. He was well known in medical circles, having been awarded a gold medal by the Royal Society of Arts for

Dr James Mounsey

the introduction of medicinal rhubarb into the country and he nad recently been made an Honoroary Member of the Royal College of Physicians in Edinburgh. It was not going to be so easy to drop out of sight completely. Doubling as his brother at his funeral might do on this occasion but he couldn't play-act that role for the rest of his life, certainly not here. He would need to leave Rammerscales for some years and the maybe return very quietly and pick up the threads again, hoping that people would have forgotten the funeral, or if they remembered it, why, it could have been another member of the family! The grave was marked only by a single sandstone cross as yet uninscribed. If people remarked on the occasion he could always say, with truth, that he'd been there himself. He almost laughed at the thought as the door opened and his servant came in with something to eat and drink.

It is not known where Dr Mounsey disappeared to for the considerable period of time that followed, but the years passed and one day in early summer a coach drew up at the front door. Dr Mounsey dismounted, leapt up the steps and disappeared into the house. Nearing seventy now, and a widower, he was nonetheless in good health and spirits — and particularly happy to be back in his beloved Rammerscales after such a long time. Or so it seemed. He was less nervous now and no longer really feared for his life, though still instinctively wary. Once assured of his surroundings he could relax completely. The house now had furniture in all the main rooms. Only the top floor was bare, and the long gallery not yet floored. The planking was still to come, which did not matter greatly as he hardly had enough furniture to put in there apart from his books and they scarcely took up half the shelf space. It was sixty feet long and ran the whole length of the south side of the house with a window at each end so that on a fine day, as this was, the sun flooded the room with warmth and light.

He went up there almost as soon as he arrived. Though it was not quite finished it was his favourite room. High up from its windows, Annandale lay below with the silver ribbon of river winding through it, all utterly peaceful. The woods and fields lay below, a patchwork of varying shades of green, broken here and there with the whitewashed farmhouses and cottages. The village clustered nearby surrounded by trees, and some distance beyond, the small town of Lockerbie nestled under the far hills that rose fold on fold and disappeared into the mist. Further to the south the line of the English hills carrying the road from Carlisle to Newcastle could be seen faintly. He laughed involuntarily at the thought of the cemetery where "Dr Mounsey" was buried, and shivered at the memory of that bitter day.

But the months went by and it gradually became known that the big house was occupied again — by a Mr James Mounsey. He had thought it advisable to drop the medical title and if people asked too many questions he would avoid giving explanations. One day he decided to take the mail coach into Edinburgh from Lochmaben. He rode in and left his horse at the Bruce Hostelry and took the "Camperdown". It was a day's run and a lovely one over the Lowther hills. They changed horses at the Brigg Inn at Beattock, again at the Crook Inn beyond Tweedsmuir and finally at Leadburn before arriving in Edinburgh that evening. He stayed at a small quiet hotel and enjoyed himself for the few days he was there. He hardly expected to be recognised until suddenly an old professor stopped him in the street near the medical faculty. "My God, Mounsey!" he exclaimed, "I thought you were dead. How pleasant to find myself in error!"

"Indeed you may have thought so," the doctor replied, "I've been away for many years, and only recently returned, and now live in the country a day's journey from our capital city."

"Ah yes," the professor continued, "Russia, wasn't it? And your claim to fame was introducing that remarkable remedy, medicinal rhubarb — it all comes back to me."

The doctor somewhat apprehensively strove to bring the conversation to a tactful conclusion before any further memories came back to the professor. They said goodbye to each other warmly and went their ways. Fortunately, Dr Mounsey was leaving the next day and he surmised that it wouldn't do to come up to Edinburgh too often, or if he did he should certainly avoid the precincts of the medical faculty. The professor had been the first outside person to recognise him . . . did it really matter, he wondered? On the whole he thought that it probably might, as his death was very likely to have been registered formally at the College of Physicians even though he had not informed them at the time he was making those elaborate arrangements for his "funeral". In fact he had felt an urge to look in the College of Physicians' files to see if his entry was still there and had been on his way when he had encountered the old professor.

The next morning he left at daybreak for the long journey back to Lochmaben.

After that expedition he rarely left Rammerscales. People did come to see him and occasionally one or other of his daughters came up from the south to stay a few days. He was well into his seventies now, and the possibility of his own death — this time for real — was never far from his mind. The chief sadness at this late stage in his life was the loss of two of his sons, one having been killed in a duel with the Marquis of Belhaven, the other dying in some fracas with the French in the West Indies. Although he was now recovered from the initial sorrow he was nonetheless anxious over his succession. Paul, his surviving son, had never had very good health, was unmarried, and would probably not willingly claim his inheritance. This left one or other of his three daughters and he rather doubted whether any of them would want to come up here to live. He had grown very fond of the old house and it grieved him to think that it would go out of his family and strangers would probably buy the place. He wondered if he would ever know — perhaps in spirit he would keep in touch with life at Rammerscales. He wouldn't want to haunt the place, he thought with smile, that sounded rather gloomy and depressing — the very word have him quite a frisson.

Often he would wander round, through some of the double doors and along the narrow passages behind the circular staircase, the top one emerging into the long gallery through a small door countersunk between the bookshelves. He smiled at the recollection of all these elaborate precautions against assassination by Russian agents. Perhaps he had exaggerated the whole thing, but it was well over now, no one was likely to want to kill him at this stage in his life. These precautions of his would no doubt amuse future generations — future generations? — whose? Once the house passed to another family nobody would ever remember who he was, what he had done, why there were all these doors and passageways. . . .

In the winter of 1773 Dr Mounsey died. Just as he had feared, his son Paul did not live long at Rammerscales and none of his daughters wished to inherit. The place was sold to a local family called Bell, two bachelor brothers, James and William, who, contrary to his fears, took the greatest interest in the old house and its surroundings.

His spirit must have watched the decades pass with increasing delight. Next to inherit was the brothers' sister, Mary, and her husband Donald Macdonald of Macdonald; this union was responsible for the change in house-name to Bell Macdonald. Donald was a scholar, a man after Dr Mounsey's own heart who had travelled extensively in his youth like himself. The old long gallery became a library — how satisfactory! It was all working out better than he had hoped. The blocking up of a passageway was of no account. Dr Mounsey could pass through it, and other walls, windows and cupboards with no difficulty and has done so on many occasions to successive generations, becoming affectionately known as "Old Jacobus".

Two incidents this century demonstrate Dr Mounsey's continuing presence at Rammerscales. Late one night an occupant of the house was, unexpectedly, still up in the library when a black form issued from one of the cupboards. "Good Lord!" he muttered in surprise at the sight of the ghostly figure dressed in black. "It must be old Jacobus!" This response was friendly and unalarmed, but on another occasion during the war, when the house was being used as a refuge from Glasgow for a teacher and some schoolchildren, the

The Library at Rammerscales with old Jacobus' door at the far end, *Scottish Field*

appearance of the ghost was too much. That very day they moved to the stables.

Another fifty years has passed but even in the last decades of the twentieth century the spirit of Dr James still pervades the old house. In fact as I write I feel him anxious to direct my pen so as to give my own account of some of the strange happenings to which he was more privy than myself.

Torosay and the Guthries

David Guthrie-James

TOROSAY CASTLE

In a report on the Hebrides some years ago, the consumer magazine *Which* concluded that Mull was the most beautiful of the islands and who am I to quarrel with that conclusion? Probably Dr Johnson would have disagreed though Sir Walter Scott, Robert Louis Stevenson, John Buchan, Felix Mendelssohn and other illustrious names associated with the island surely would not.

Historically the parish of Torosay extended from Salen down to Ardura and was part of the living of the Abbots of Iona. It then became clan territory of the Macleans of Duart until it was forfeit to the more powerful Campbells, Dukes of Argyll, in 1688. Later, after the rising of '45, Duart Castle was first inhabited by redcoats and ultimately blown up.

No one could deny that the choicest spot on the island is Duart Bay at its south-eastern tip, where the Sound of Mull enters between Lismore Lighthouse and the ruined castle on the point. There, snugly sited at the head of the bay, stands Torosay Castle, built by David Bryce in the Guthrie "Scottish Baronial" style in 1865 on the former site of a small farmhouse that no longer accorded with the lifestyle of Victorian lairds. With the point as foreground it commands a view of the whole Appin range of hills from Ben Cruachan behind Oban right up to Ben Nevis, beyond Fort William and thirty-six miles distant. It is also sheltered by hills and woodlands from all quarters bar the north-east, which is why some of our hardwoods that ring the garden are so long-lived and hence larger than most on the stormy western seaboard.

The Guthries were an ancient but never numerous clan that came from a place of that name near Forfar in what is now Angus at the head of the Vale of Strathmore, where stands Guthrie Castle to this day. By repute the earliest one was Falconer to King Malcolm Canmore (d. 1093) but owing to clan feuds and English invasions which led to the destruction of family records, we cannot trace our ancestry back with certainty for more than eighteen generations to Alexander Guthrie, living in 1465. His son and one grandson fell at the Field of Flodden in 1513 but then, after the usual vicissitudes that befell families that survived the Reformation, the Civil War, and the Jacobite rebellions, with their lands intact (invariably by someone being on the winning side at the end of the day!) they settled down respectably as lairds, ministers of religion or merchants. Such a one was David Charles Guthrie (1778-1859) of Craigie, scion of the other arms-bearing branch of the family, who set up in business in Dundee as a merchant adventurer with Patrick Chalmers, a neighbour. The business prospered and soon they moved down to Idol Lane in London, hard by St Paul's Cathedral.

He had two sons, James Alexander, born at Craigie in 1823, and Arbuthnot Guthrie, born in London two years later, and both entered the family business. Unfortunately, they fell in love with the same girl, the beautiful Ellinor, daughter of Admiral Sir James Stirling, the founder of Perth, Western Australia. In the end the elder of the two brothers won her favour and this is what impelled my great-grand-uncle to cut his losses and in 1865, buy Torosay and its 14,000-acre estate for the huge sum of £90,000. But no sooner had he done so than he got cold feet and wanted to sell it again, which would not have suited his brother's books at all. So in the autumn of 1865, James came up to see for himself what his brother had bought. The letter he wrote from the Great Western Hotel in Oban gives us an interesting appreciation of the times.

They had gone by train to Inverness and then got a "swift boat" down the Caledonian Canal to Oban. On Friday 28th, they chartered a small cutter for ten shillings which landed them at Salen, from where they got a dog-cart down to Craignure, and as the Craignure Inn could not hold such a large party, they got rooms prepared for them at the castle. The next day they drove down to Ardura and found "the scenery beautiful . . . road pretty good, land capable of improvement". Both James and his wife were "delighted with the place; the house is as good as any man could wish — only too good: Grounds pretty and everything about the place perfect — requiring no more money to be laid out — only to be kept in order. There is a gardener and he has two apprentices at £5 a year each, meal and milk which he says are enough to do the work properly: There is only one gamekeeper and a sort of watcher . . . says you may at the beginning of the season get ten brace of grouse a day or maybe ten brace of blackgame in the woods; in the winter no end of duck and he has seen twenty one couple of woodstock shot in a day. . . ."

Apparently there were only about fifty red deer at the time but they "saw a fellow Maclaine who told Kennedy there were four stags and one hind close to his cottage". They were also informed that Maclaine was "about the only dangerous man on the place and that *sometimes he eats deer flesh*"! There followed a list of servants who were worth keeping as necessary for the place. Curie, the gamekeeper, got £45 a year, a pint of milk per day or a cow's grazing and seven tons of coal a year. The forester got £40 per year, a ploughman £24 and the gardener fourteen shillings a week but wanted a rise to seventeen shillings. In addition there was a fisherman, and a sawman who attended the gasometer used for lighting which used fourteen tons of coal a year costing £1 per ton with an additional 45 tons of domestic coal for the house and staff at

View of Torosay Castle

about twelve shillings a ton, landed on the beach.

James was entirely happy with his trip until it was time to leave. They had to wait nearly an hour on the old stone pier (built as famine relief work in 1849 when the Irish potato blight hit Scotland also). They then had to go on board a passing steamer in a small boat, though he cheered himself up by saying the situation would be alleviated by lengthening the pier to let the steamer come alongside. As a matter of interest, it was ninety years before a new pier was built for this purpose. He was appalled, though, by the price paid for the place but consoled himself with the thought that once the railroad was finished to Oban, daily summer communication up the Sound of Mull would soon follow and it would then rise in value.

Such was Torosay where Arbuthnot Guthrie and his plain wife Anne spent the greater part of each year for thirty-two years. For some unknown reason, though, they changed the name from Torosay Castle, which it had been called by its builder, to Duart House, taking over the name of the ruin on the point. We know little of their mode of life as only one or two photographs remain. Great-aunt Vi (the Hon. Mrs Stuart-Mortley), my grandfather's last surviving sister, published her memoirs *Grow Old Along With Me* in her old age in the early 1950s and gives us some interesting glimpses:

> "That summer I spent a few weeks in Mull, where my uncle Arbuthnot Guthrie owned a lovely place on the extreme point of the island, facing Oban. The comparatively modern house was built in what is called Scotch-baronial style, that is, pepper-boxy on the outside, and the interior Landseerish. There were, as decorations, stags' antlers, and large trout in glass cases. This did not spoil one's delight in staying there, because the surrounding scenery is incomparably beautiful. A yacht anchored in the bay, and the weather, capricious but fairly dependable in August, enabled the friends gathered there to sail (or steam) east or west exploring the coast along the the island or the mainland. We spent the time pleasantly picnicking on rocky shores in the company of seals, fishing by torch-light, when the shoals of herring churned up the waters of the bay, or off the point during the long afternoons with rod and line and bait. The uncle was a queer fellow. A collector of first-rate objets d'art and although prepared to pay thousands of pounds for a piece of furniture, he practised

niggardly economies, very annoying to guests. Returning from a sale of the Hamilton Palace treasures, where against spirited bidding he had secured two commodes at £10,000 apiece, he caused his hungry family the maximum anxiety over the dish placed before him for carving. How in the world would he make two grouse furnish an adequate repast for six or seven anticipatory diners? With extraordinary skill he managed it, that is to say that each one at the table got something on his or her plate; the ghost of a dinner! To the younger members of the party it was a tantalising experience. But, apart from this idiosyncrasy, there was such warmth of feeling in the uncle's uncommunicativeness, that the nieces and nephews loved him."

About great-aunt Anne, his wife, she was somewhat less enthusiastic.

"Awaiting him at home for luncheon was his elderly wife, clad in voluminous garments, a black silk apron tied where her waist had been, a cap covering a chevelure already rapidly thinning and, as pin to the ruche round her already sagging neck, a sapphire known in the family as the Mediterranean Sea, so large was it and so deeply blue."

She was a sister of Field Marshal Sir Neville Chamberlain who had been Lord Roberts' commanding officer in the Indian Mutiny and, when Lord Roberts was home on his rare leaves from India, he frequently dined with the Guthries in their London house, a fact I elicited when I wrote Lord Roberts' definitive biography. But she bore him no children and can have been no consolation to him for his adored Ellinor, whom he could never bring himself to meet again except once after his brother's early death in 1873.

Arbuthnot Guthrie died in February 1897, leaving about £960,000 (some £34 million in 1985 money terms). He left the contents of Torosay to his terrible widow Anne, who promptly decamped to London, taking everything with her except the dining-room sideboard which was too big to get out of the door. (This was a pity as we could have done with the Landseers and Hamilton Palace commodes!) However, after this due provision for his widow who had a London house anyway, he left the residue in exactly equal proportions to his three nephews and six nieces. My grandfather, Murray, got an empty castle and the estate, together with a steam

Murray Guthrie in 1909, *Sargent*

yacht, two houses on the front in Oban and shares in the Oban and Callender Railway Company, which was considered equivalent of what the others got. So for the first but by no means the last time Torosay was passed on without supportive cash.

Life at the turn of the century must have looked very promising to Walter Murray Guthrie. He was by repute the best looking young man about town and very rich. In 1892, on coming down from Cambridge, where he had been bone idle but founded and edited *The Granta*, he had been accepted straightaway as a partner in Chalmers Guthrie which, apart from much else, had become the biggest importer of coffee into the United Kingdom. In 1895 he had married Olive, the beautiful youngest daughter of Sir John Leslie, Bart. of Glaslough, Co. Monaghan; and the old man, who had just given up being an MP, gave them his London home as part of her dowry. This was Stratford House (now the Oriental Club) and Murray set about improving it.

Then unexpectedly he was left Torosay. Being appalled at this burden, he promptly put it on the market. The terms of offer still survive and are in a bound volume for all to read: "Substantial and commodious mansion adapted for a family of rank". The sporting characteristics were varied and unique and "presented a combination of attractions seldom united to such an extent in any single property, offering to a Capitalist (sic) and lover of sport an almost unparalleled opportunity of indulging his energetic proclivities". All this now jars as much as great-aunt Vi's description of the house as being "pepper-boxy" but different generations have different perceptions and it is as well to see oneself as seen by others. At a more practical level, the estate was of 24,233 acres, or thirty-seven square miles, with fifteen miles of coastline and there were eight farms, sixteen crofts and more than twenty-five other dwellings including the school, village shop and inn with a rent-roll of £3,600 a year. So it was a lovely inheritance and at that time, before the decline in sheep-farming, self-supporting.

In the spring, Murray and Olive came up to look at the place. It was at its loveliest so they took it off the market at once. Further, Murray immediately consulted Sir Robert Lorimer, best known for his War Memorial in Edinburgh Castle, to help him effect his scheme for connecting the castle to the old walled garden which was some 120 yards away, by three levels of Italianate terraces. When it became apparent that the central line of the old garden did not run

The Torosay Statues

true in relation to the opened-up alignment of the house, he extended it back in a straight line on the western side and created a Statue Walk. For this purpose he went out to Italy and found a derelict villa garden on the outskirts of Milan containing nineteen life-size peasant figures by Antonio Bonazza (1698-1763), which he acquired for a song. They came back as ballast in a tramp-steamer from Genoa and I always remember my grandmother telling me that the most expensive part of the operation was getting them up from the Clyde by "puffer" and then by farm-cart to their plinths, as each weighed three-quarters of a ton. Further, over again to the west, he damned up the mill-lade to create a water-garden in a dell. For just two weeks in May-June when the rhodies, the azaleas, the clematis and the bluebells are out simultaneously, it is like paradise.

On October 27th, 1899, Murray was returned as Conservative M.P. for Bow and Bromley in a by-election which turned on the conduct of the Boer War. His campaign posters decorate a tearoom here and show that in the eyes of the time, this was viewed as a battle against apartheid — albeit white apartheid of Uitlander against Boer. Six months later he was joined in the House by his friend Winston Churchill. Olive's older brother Jack had married Leonie, the youngest of the three Jerome sisters, the oldest of course being

Lady Randolph Churchill. During his neglected childhood, Winston spent much time sharing a nursery with my grandmother to whom he was still sending affectionate messages fifty years later when Prime Minister. Unhappily, the third Jerome sister married one Morton Frewin, known to all as Mortal Ruin, as all his schemes failed. Murray lost quite a lot by backing one of them called the Sulphide Trust, which came to nothing.

Those first ten summers at Torosay were the golden ones as the visitors' book makes clear: Admiral Lord Charles Beresford (Olive's cousin), Winston Chrurchill (shot his first stag Sept. 10th 1899), Jennie Randolph Churchill and her future second husband George Conwallis-West, F. C. Selous (author and big-game hunter), Nellie Melba (opera singer), Jeanne Langtry (daughter of "Jersey Lily"), Edward Poynter PRA, A. E. W. Mason (author of *The Four Feathers*), Admiral Prince Louis of Battenburg (later Lord Milford Haven and father of Earl Mountbatten), Dr Axel Munthe (Swedish doctor and author of *The Story of San Michele*), and Faith Cellie (actress) to name but a few.

And then this glittering world started to collapse because both Murray's health and his business faltered. So far as his health was concerned, diabetes was diagnosed which was then incurable, so there started a long series of trips to spas seeking a cure. In 1906, he had to give up Bow and Bromley taking with him a gracious tribute from his opponent and successor, George Lansbury, later to lead the Labour Party: "If there were more like you, there would be fewer like me". Two years later he had to give up his aldermanic seat, which was a pity as he would otherwise have been the youngest ever Lord Mayor of London.

Chalmers Guthrie was always a high risk business and had been in difficulty before. The first time was in 1840 when the economy of Mauritius nearly collapsed and the partners had much money invested in financing sugar plantations. James Alexander's first job on coming down from Oxford was to go out there where he had to foreclose on a number of properties. It was the profit on these, when things recovered, that enabled Uncle Buth to buy Torosay. There was further trouble in Hong Kong in 1867 when Lyall, Still & Company failed, owing the partners the huge sum of £574,686 of which £134,000 14s 4d had ultimately to be written off.

It was this second blow which turned their attention to Central America, at first with very considerable success; but political instability following the Spanish-American War and a virtual currency collapse deprived them of their main export market almost overnight so they couldn't finance the coffee imports. This crisis escalated at such a rate that in 1907 Murray had to mortgage Torosay for £58,000 to provide extra working capital. This saved the day but by this time his health was going fast. To cap it all, in 1910, the mortgagee (a relative who shall be nameless) sought to foreclose on him. He wrote back angrily, saying if he wanted to do so he should do it at once while he yet had time to make other arrange-ments and not await his death. Luckily his personal standing in the City still stood high and when he approached his friend Sir Ernest Cassel, he promptly made an arrangement which averted the crisis and he was able to die peacefully in April 1911. A week before his death he had sold back Duart Castle and the Point to the Chief of the Clan Maclean, who was thus able to restore his heritage. So Torosay reverted to its original name, a fact that has been confusing visitors ever since, as there are things such as leather blotting pads and a game register with Duart stamped on them, which we are assumed to have filched from our neighbours!

Some months later, a friend, Filton Young, wrote of him in the old *Saturday Review*: "There was nothing commonplace about this last year. The scene was changed from that London element in which he had moved so smoothly and so surely to one place of cure after another, and finally to his home on the island of Mull, where the last stand was made and the final triumph achieved. It was a strange destiny for Murray Guthrie that he who had been girded for the battle of public affairs should be thrust at the last into the arena of purely spiritual conflict."

For the next thirty-three years the story of Torosay is of a long and skilful rearguard action. Against my grandmother was the fact that she was chronically short of capital and that her sons did not prove to be of much practical assistance. Pat, the elder, idled in Paris at the age of thirty-seven, never having got over his experience in the war. In the words of a kindly obituary notice, "the business life did not appeal to him". So Chalmers Guthrie wilted away and died. Another minus was that my grandmother maintained the tradition of never leaving anyone on the estate without a job, so even if the wages were pitifully low, there were always people for whom work had to be found. The wife of Mackechnie, the shepherd, for example, bore him thirteen children, all of whom were taken on in one capacity or another. At one time, three of them were employed in and around the garage which seemed even then to be a little excessive for one car and a truck.

On the positive side was first her own sheer guts, plus an enormous amount of charm. There were always, therefore, friends and relations ready to give an over-the-top rental for sporting lets. For two consecutive seasons, her nephew, Jackie Crawshay, took the stalking and then gave us back all the stags as his guests! Then there was still quite a lot of surplus fat, and over the years about 8,000 acres of low ground was sold in bits and pieces to the Forestry Commission. Finally, her married daughters, my mother and my aunt, with their families, were always a source of strength so that the house in summer was still full of happy laughing people as in the old days.

Before the war came, my grandmother made over the main estate to my mother, and Auchencraig, a self-contained peninsula, to my aunt, retaining for herself just the castle and its eleven acres of garden. So all was turning out well except each year that passed left the place looking that little bit dowdier. This process was, of course, accelerated by the war which took away what little labour was left. Thus the lawns were not mown and hedges remained untrimmed. Then, apart from our rare wartime leaves, only her suite and the library were ever open or even dusted, and fungus started growing out of a wall in the central hall. All meals were taken in common in the servants' hall, which was both warm and sensible, and I recollect vividly that when I got back from a lucky escape from a German POW camp we had a 6 p.m. feast of stewed rabbit, strong tea and champagne, leaving my grandmother, John Bill the old butler, and myself, distinctly unsteady on our feet.

In January 1945, I managed to get myself appointed to the Antarctic and it was there, in July, that I received a telegram informing me of my grandmother's death, and also that I had been left the castle and gardens — but, once again, with no cash! She had also directed that her ashes should be interred in Murray's grave and that John Bill should carry the urn. She could not have foreseen that it would take two men to carry John Bill but that would have delighted her Irish spirit. Her departure just after the end of the war in Europe but before VJ Day was well timed in that no one seriously

Constance Leslie 18th August 1897 —

John Leslie.

Charles Beresford. Sept. 13th 1897.

Jennie Randolph Churchill Sept 7th " } married 1900

G. Cornwallis-West " " "

Winston S. Churchill. Sept. 10th 1899. (Killed his first stag)

F. C. Selous. Jan 16th 1901. Killed in action S.W. Africa 1916.

Nellie Melba Sept 18th 1901

Jeanne Langtry October 1st 1901.

Edward J. Poynter.

A. E. W. Mason

Louis Battenberg Vice Admiral 28 June 1909

Axel Munthe 22 July – Aug 1.

Faith Celli May 3rd – May 10th

Elisabeta 4 – 11 Sept 1930

George R " "

Hugh Ruttledge May 23-24, 1935.

Winston S. Churchill.

Torosay first visited by Concorde's sonic-boom 5.47-5.48 pm Sept 1st 1970

Extracts from the Visitors' Book.

believed that I could ever live in Torosay on a naval lieutenant's pay so that the castle and contents were accepted for probate at £1,000.

I got back the following summer to find that my stepfather, Geoffrey Miller, had come out of the army and that he and my mother were living in Java Lodge, the dower house in Craignure. I discovered that they had re-engaged a gardener at the then shocking rate of £4 a week and had cleared the main drain down from the well of the roof (which put an end to the fungus) and carried out bare minimal repairs, and then let the place to a dear old couple whose dream had always been to run an hotel and who had renamed the place the "Tangle of the Isles"! It rapidly became known as "The Tangle" as that is exactly what it was but after two years it went bust, so I took it on myself. I was only twenty-seven at the time and it did not take me long to find out that I lacked business experience and that architecturally Torosay just wasn't adaptable to the role owing to the large size of the bedrooms and lack of private bathrooms. That epoch had, however, enabled us to get building licences for essential work when there would not otherwise have been obtainable.

To pay off the debt on the roof, my mother and Geoffrey sold Java and moved back in again. So yet another chapter had started. They soon found it was too cold in winter, being without any form of heating. They therefore converted the old kitchen-wing into a ground level flat with sitting room, dining room, kitchen, three bedrooms and two bathrooms. At first they were going to come upstairs again every summer but, predictably, only did so once, as they were too snug below.

By this time I had married Jaquetta, the youngest daughter of the eleventh Baron Digby. Her eldest sister had been married to Randolph Churchill, so young Winston was her nephew, thus providing a further Churchill link. I worked in London so the main part of the house was only opened up in the summer for my mother's guests and my annual three weeks' holiday. Since the walls ran with condensation all winter, this meant that my mother had to distemper them herself every spring and at one time there were almost one hundred buckets and cans in the attics to catch the drips. During the following twenty years, which saw my wife and I having six children and my being elected to Parliament in 1959, ejected in 1964, and re-elected in 1970, my mother and Geoffrey laboured heroically to keep the gardens going on their own and without help, while I conducted the stalking for as long as I could afford to. These were busy days but happy ones too with my mother never losing an opportunity to throw a dance or a party.

In 1964 my mother and I jointly made over the castle and the estate in Discretionary Trust between my four sons. By 1973, I became convinced we couldn't carry on our rather hot pace indefinitely, so I commissioned a report on estate policy from Strutt & Parker's Edinburgh office. This came up with the idea, confirmed by their leisure department the following year, that so far from trying to support the castle from estate revenue, the boot should be on the other foot and we should open our doors to the public. This has opened the latest chapter in the Torosay saga.

It was in 1964 that the real change came when the completion of the new pier in Craignure meant that instead of one daily sailing from Oban to Tobermory carrying four cars, we at once had the potential for six daily sailings taking four hundred cars. So, in 1973, we tentatively opened our doors and were surprised that nearly 2,000 people paid five shillings to see round. It was all very amateurish, of course, with someone sitting at a card-table in the front hall to take the money, and cups of tea in our own kitchen. There were not even any guidebooks or postcards on sale, but people seemed pleased enough. That winter we turned the old laundry into a proper tearoom and converted my grandmother's suite into two archive rooms plus toilet facilities. We also erected a wooden reception office plus a shop outside the front gate so that we nearly doubled the number of rooms open and our numbers trebled. With a decent guidebook and a selection of postcards, plus goods for sale on commission, our receipts quadrupled. All the signs now pointed strongly in one direction. . . .

To restore a rundown place one needs both the will and the resources, and thus encouraged we found both. There was still one area we could sell to the Forestry Commission without damage to the estate, and that had to go, but with Mull's growing popularity we found an increasing demand for land for retirement homes. Aided by generous grants from the Scottish Buildings Council and the HIDB, and more recently, ploughed-back receipts, we have by now been able to underpin the foundations with concrete to prevent further subsidence, rebuild two leaning gable-ends, reslate the roof, renew the tower lead platform and rewire the whole place. All these things were necessary and expensive but hardly satisfying either to our visitors or to ourselves. It's a different story now that we have made a start on redecorating reception rooms and restoring and polishing furniture.

The same can be said about the garden, where much of the work has been undertaken by my stepfather, as one terrace wall had to be rebuilt for its entire length and flying buttresses and arches had to be reconstructed or repointed. But now there is a new colonnade in the walled garden built of marble pillars my grandfather had bought but never used, and a new Japanese Garden to the east opening views up Loch Linnhe to Ben Nevis. After one hundred and fifity years standing in the open in Lombardy and a further ninety years in Argyll, the statues needed attention too, as we learnt that they are the most important eighteenth-century collection outside Italy. So nine of them have spent the winter in London being cleaned and having a water resistant substance added to their limestone. As this costs £2,500 for each statue it is proving harder to fund as garden statuary seems to be outwith the terms of any grant-giving body. So we were grateful to the lady who last summer sent us £1,000 because she had fallen in love with them.

I came out of Parliament in 1979, as it was obviously becoming impossible to do justice to a constituency and an historic home five hundred miles apart. From then on we spent the summer up here but the winters down south as we still had one son whose education

One of the Statues by Antonio Bonazza of Venice (1698-1765)

was not yet complete. In April 1983, we came back for keeps, bringing with us a lot of Torosay furniture we had "liberated" on our marriage thirty-three years before when we never thought to see the place fully furnished again. By a melancholy coincidence, that month saw the disposal of the contents of Guthrie Castle which had just had to be sold after more than five hundred years. In the same week also, Craigie, which had been swallowed up by Dundee and long been an old folk's home, was demolished by the local authority who found it would be cheaper to purpose-build something new. For these obvious reasons I assumed the additional name of Guthrie, matriculating the arms of Guthrie-James of Torosay to differentiate them from those of Craigie registered in 1772.

Between 1975 and 1983, our number of visitors rose slowly from 2,000 to 20,000. Then last year, aided by a miniature railway which now runs from Craignure to within 250 yards of the house, we shot up to 28,817, so we view the beginning of our second decade in a mood of optimism. We still occasionally get asked whether we don't resent people wandering round our home but we feel that is what a house like this should be for and we meet charming and appreciative people from all over the world. Torosay has always had a very happy atmosphere, as people so often kindly remark, and the more lovely we can make it the more that will be enhanced and the happier we will be too.

ADDRESSES AND OPENING TIMES

ARBIGLAND, Kirkbean, Dumfriesshire DG2 8BQ
house open 20 days a year. Telephone (038 788) 283. Garden open May to September. Tuesday, Thursday and Sunday .200 p.m.-6.00 p.m.

ARDCHATTAN PRIORY, Connel, Argyll PA37 1RQ
Gardens and Chapel open 9.30 a.m.-5.30 p.m. House open 1st and 2nd Sunday in August for organised parties by prior arrangement. Telephone (0631 175) 274.

BEMERSYDE, Melrose, Roxburghshire TD6 9DP
Not open to the public.

CARESTON CASTLE, Brae of Pert, Laurencekirk,
Kincardineshire AB3 1QR
Open only for charity or for special parties. Telephone Estate Office, Northwaterbridge (067484) 206. After hours: Brechin (035 62) 2985.

CAWDOR CASTLE, Nairn, Scotland IV12 5RD
Castle and Gardens open May to September, 10.00 a.m.-5.30 p.m.
Telephone (06677) 615.

CRAIGSTON CASTLE, Turriff, Aberdeenshire
Open only by appointment. Also at certain times in the summer. Telephone (088 85) 228.

EILEAN AIGAS, Kiltarlity, by Beauly, Inverness-shire
Not open to the public.

FINLAYSTONE, Langbank, Renfrewshire PA14 6TJ
Woods and Gardens open all year round. Home open on Sunday afternoons in summer. Other visits to house possible by appointment; meals can be arranged. Telephone (047 554) 285.

GILMERTON HOUSE, Haddington, East Lothian
Not open to the public.

GLENTRUIM HOUSE, by Newtonmore, Inverness-shire
Can be visited by special request. Telephone (054 03) 221.

HADDO HOUSE
Open 1st May-30th September, 2.00 p.m.-6.00 p.m. ever day. Gardens open throughout the year. Telephone (06515) 440.

HARDEN, Hawick, Roxburghshire TD9 7LP
Visits by appointment only. Telephone (0450) 72069.

RAMMERSCALES, Lockerbie, Dumfriesshire DG11 1LD
Open certain days end of July to beginning of September 1987. For details see local press or telephone (038 781) 361.

TOROSAY CASTLE, Craignure, Isle of Mull
Open from 1st May until end of September; April and October by appointment. Telephone (06802) 421. Gardens open all year.